Portchester In Living Memory
~ Foreword ~

OUR THOUGHTS ON 'ORAL HISTORY' started in the old Parish Hall on the corner of White Hart Lane and Castle Street in November 2001, when the newly formed Portchester Civic Society was holding its first 'Memories of Portchester' exhibition. A resident of Portchester, whose family goes back generations running a bakery and general store in Castle Street, held a story corner at the exhibition. Edgar Long sat there all day talking about his family history to an enthralled audience. We felt that this history should not be forgotten and set about finding a way of recording these memories before they were lost forever.

With the enthusiastic help of Bryan Jerrard, who took on the management of this project, this book has been produced by The Portchester Civic Society. Generously funded by the Heritage Lottery Fund and a grant from Fareham Borough Council, it is an attempt to re-tell some of Portchester's story through the memories of more than sixty local people.

Their recollections have been recorded by a group of Society members, trained for the purpose in a technique known as 'oral history', then transcribed. Edited by Bryan Jerrard and illustrated by Paul Woodman from the large library of pictures held by The Society, these memories cover a period of over ninety years, in the strong belief that everyone has a story to tell about their life. Included here are not just the seniors who recall the First World War, but teenagers at college and children at school, with experiences that are very different from those even of their parents. The young are a valid part of the history of Portchester. We take the area of our research as the political boundary up to the Delme roundabout rather than the parish boundary and we have gone outside those boundaries to meet some contributors.

Many readers will hear on the radio and see on television the very many occasions that the memories of the past are valuable and even riveting, and are often quoted; we hope that you will find this compilation of excerpts from the recordings an interesting addition to Portchester's story.

Hazel Woodman
Chairman, The Portchester Civic Society
March 2007

Portchester –
An Historical Introduction

PORTCHESTER'S STORY BEGAN in Stone Age times with settlers in the Red Barn area on Portsdown Hill. But it was the Romans who left their mark when they built a defensive fort at the end of the promontory into what became Portsmouth's harbour. The site was later occupied by Saxons and the area attacked by Vikings. The Roman fort was settled by Norman builders of the Augustinian Priory Church of St Mary's and the 12th century Castle.

The Castle hosted visits by medieval kings – notably John of Magna Carta fame – who sometimes repaired, enlarged and embellished it and used it as a military base. Royal demands for iron, weapons, fuel and food stimulated local trade and the growth of the small population. The Castle constable administered one of the three manors of Portchester. Medieval records show details of Portchester's tenants, the rents they paid and the extra work demanded at harvest time. Broadly, one of the three medieval fields was north of the modern A27. The Middle Field was south of the A27 to the track that became White Hart Lane. South Field extended to the coast and included marsh-land. Each was divided into strips often a furrow long – a furlong. Sea-water fed the salt pans, the Downs encouraged sheep grazing and the Forest of Bere provided timber.

When Henry VII set up a Royal dockyard in Portsmouth in the 1490s, Portchester's role as a secure sea base declined. In Elizabethan times its population was too few and too poor to repair its parish church without a Royal grant. Later, during Dutch wars in the 1650s and European wars in the 1700s, Castle and Church were used as a prison. At this time Portchester House was used as a hospital and thus gave its name to Hospital Lane.

In Republican and Napoleonic Wars thousands of prisoners were held in the Castle. Their artistic skills may be admired in exhibits in Westbury Manor Museum in Fareham. Some local families claim ancestry from French officers billeted with families. Several homes were once inns; the *Cormorant* in South Street, now Castle Street, seems to have been purpose built as a coaching inn from about 1815.

About this time the common fields were enclosed into large fields and compact holdings. The principal specialism for the next 150 years was market gardening for local, urban markets. Geology and access favoured this. Census listings reflect this occupational bias showing both family owners and employees.

Imported clay from Cornwall for pipe making and the railway's arrival in 1848 provided some work. In the 1880s the large Hayter family, keen Methodists, built wagons, carts, coffins and later, motor bodies.

Victorian life for some was short. Burial records at St Mary's suggest that the average age at death for males in the 1880s was 50 years and for females 43 years. Some poor ended their days in the Fareham workhouse.

From earlier times a day-school and Sunday school, and in the 1870s, Castle Street Board School, provided some regular education but census records indicate

Portchester IN LIVING MEMORY

a very limited range of job opportunities. Many men followed a naval or military career and women often went into service.

Portchester was a favourite destination for visitors from Portsmouth and Southsea who came by rail and sea to enjoy the environment and tea-rooms. But Portchester's population had declined in Victorian times to 888 in 1901 and it remained under 1,000 in the 1921 census. Portchester is still referred to by many as 'the village'. But housing developments in the 1920s, mostly south of the old A27, doubled the population to over 2,000 by 1931. The semi-detached bungalows cost about £400 when White Hart Lane was an unmetalled track across market gardens. These were the very early days of piped water, sewage, gas and electricity – and council housing after the 1st World War. During the 1939-1945 war, stray bombs killed some residents in West Street, damaged housing elsewhere and hastened the days when many homeless families from Portsmouth benefited from the post-war housing expansion. Portchester quadrupled in size to 9,400 by 1951 and house building up the slopes of Portsdown

Hill continued at a pace with in-fill housing south of the A27 main road. By 1971 about one half of the present housing stock on the hill had been built, some by the well known local firm of Sturgess, another Methodist family. Other builders recognising increased prosperity provided car parking.

In the last thirty years, the population has risen to nearly 18,000 – the mid-census estimate of 2006 by Hampshire County Council – with attendant housing, new primary schools, new health centres and a new library. Meeting the demands of a growing population has encouraged the development of the community centre and sports and recreational facilities. High tech enterprises on industrial estates provide work for locals. A pedestrianised precinct with national and independent retailers serves local shoppers away from traffic, diverted from West and East Streets to a new A27. Instead of residential police, new beat arrangements include bicycles and squad cars. The four churches – St Mary's, the Methodist, the Catholic and the Free Church – work and witness together. There is a profusion of clubs and societies including a social club from the 1920s and some time-honoured pubs. In June each year the popular gala reflects the whole life of the community in the grounds of the Castle. And people return to Portchester to retire where many well-known families can trace their pedigrees back for generations.

Bryan Jerrard

Fiona Taylor, née Whiting, of Canterbury, at the grave of her great-grandparents in St. Mary's graveyard. The Whiting family has been connected to Portchester since 1198.

Chapter One –
Longest Memories of Portchester

STAN HAYTER
I was born 10th August 1908. I can actually remember my mother and father looking at the *Daily Mirror*, in those days we didn't have a radio of course, and talking about the seriousness of war breaking out.

Castle Street School was the only school I went to. Mr Bennett was there when I first went but I don't think he stayed long before we had a Mr Brooks.

My grandfather [William Hayter, apprenticed in 1871, aged 17, as a wheelwright] had a motorbike and sidecar and he often used to take me in to Fareham, never far afield.

When I was a lad I used to do a newspaper round and in those days newspapers came out from Portsmouth by train. I used to go to the station to meet the train to collect the papers and I got to know the signalman down there. Mr Leach, the stationmaster, asked me if I would like to be on the railway because they had a vacancy at Portchester for a lad in the office, and that is how I came to work on the railway in 1922. I went from an office lad to a porter at Long Parish, Andover, on about 5/- a week [25p]. My wife's mother had a room in Spencer and Penn's, the shoe shop, and I lived just across in West Street.

I stayed on the railway. I went to West Moors, then Gosport as a grade 1 porter. I got 50/- a week [£2.50]. I got a house in Castle Street, no 82.

RUBY FRANKUM
I was born in Station Road in 1922. My father had come back from the First World War minus a leg. He volunteered as a Territorial and he was in the Horse Artillery and he went to France and Egypt and Salonika. He lived at West End House, which was his father's business, which were painters of signs, wheelwrights and coachbuilders. Grandfather Hayter had ten children, six sons and four daughters and all his sons worked for him, but eventually one of the sons, Alfred Hayter,

went on his own and he was the one that had all the garages all along the south coast. The other sons worked for their father as wheelwrights and sign writers and they made all the carts for the farmers around here.

A.E. Hayter & Sons display of Allen Scythes in the yard behind Hayter's Garage, early 1950s. Allen Scythes were used for cutting rough and long grass on fields, orchards and rough ground and would have been popular with the market gardeners in the Portchester area at the time.

Father bought an old army hut and converted it into a house for us and we lived in there. Very primitive! They brought up four children there. My mother worked up at 'The Mount' for Sir Harold and Lady Pink. He was the Lord Mayor of Portsmouth during the First World War. Father kept pigs. My first job was at a draper's in Fareham at 5/- [25p] a week.

JOHN TOWSE
My grandmother's sister married the original Hayter and he had a lot of children.

KATHLEEN WELLS
At school in the 1920s. We did…ballet. I can't do that now!

LESLEY PEARCE
I was born in 1913 on Red Barn Farm, a market garden growing vegetables, peas, mostly vegetables sold to Portsmouth. It stretched up to near Fort Nelson right down to the railway line. Later we moved to 76 West Street. It was mostly a dairy farm, Friesians, mixed cows with meadows that stretched nearly down to the Castle, on the east side of the Castle. My father started up with his two step-brothers. My brother took over the milk round. I had a bicycle with a milk churn on one side and a bucket on the other and you served it with measures until bottles were brought in. I went

out twice a day. In the afternoon it was a different area. All round Newtown and all round Portchester, Station Road and that.

My father was laid up and had to go to the hospital, he lost his leg during the war and of course he couldn't do any more ground work. He sold up in 1932.

I then went into building work and progressed to foreman on several sites. Different sites, different trades and I am more or less a multi tradesman and later became a site foreman. The first one I worked for was a man by the name of Mundy. I worked for him for about two years. He was a First World War man. I helped to build Newtown old people's properties and houses in Highlands Road, Fareham, in Crookhorn and Horndean and some work out near Arundel at Yapton.

Red Barn Farm. The Hayward family farmed here.

My mother died in the 1918 flu epidemic. It was a terrible death. When she died I was five years old.

I remember a Zeppelin in the War. It came across the Red Barn and we were out watching it and I was only 4 or 5 years old. You could see the people then. It went up between the two forts, Fort Nelson and Fort Southwick.

VIC RESTALL [born in 1913]

We moved here on Good Friday, 1939 to a bungalow in Denville Avenue. Right down to the shore and right over to the Castle was all open farm land. This place cost £425. We paid £25 down and 1/10 [9p] a week rates. There were no drains; every other house had a cess pit. The cess pit was next door and was cleared about every five to six weeks.

BARBARA CURTIS [born in 1915]

The very first things I can remember are when I was about 4, we had some sheep on the farm and it was lambing time. We were in the rick yard with the shepherd who was a very nice chap and a very good shepherd, he was rather monosyllabic, he didn't do a lot of talking. There was a ewe on the ground and not looking very well and I said 'Shepherd, I don't like the look of the ewe'. No notice was taken. No reply. 'Why don't you do something?' He turned round and looked on the ground and there was a lamb. The shepherd said ' I reckon she'll feel a bit better now don't you?' That was the first animal I had ever seen born – on Murrill's Farm. It belonged to the Thistlethwaite Estate and was quite large. It went all along the main road. It was a mixed farm, wheat, oats, barley and roots for the animals. There was another farm, Sturgess's Farm, next door to us. We had about five cows. The farm was sold when I was about eight or nine and most people bought their own farms. My father bought what was the farm that ran up to the top of Portsdown Hill and down to the main road.

Barbara Curtis, pictured in 2005, grew up at Murrill's Farm.

We had two Miss Bakers as governesses. One was excellent, she was brilliant. She taught us about money, all the county towns of Hampshire, all about the Thames, Portsmouth Harbour, Southampton Water, Poole Bay, all the way to Cornwall.

I took my school certificate at Portsmouth High School in Kent Road. I went there when I was nine with my sister by bus. It was an ordinary school certificate. The headmistress wanted me to go to University. I took history and she gave me special tutoring. I went to Cambridge [in 1933] which was a very big mistake because I was not a suitable subject to live in an institution. We had a wonderful Professor Clapham, he was a wonderful man. There were a few lovely ladies who had gone just for the ride. They didn't do any work and at the end of the term they left. Then we had the sporting maniacs. I played netball and lacrosse at school so I decided to row. River rowing at Cambridge is one thing in October and November; sea rowing — I had done a lot of rowing at home — is another. I was used to the 'ducks' [a locally designed sailing boat] at Portchester. I was at Cambridge for two terms but my parents wasted a lot of money for nothing. They said you had better clear off so I got a job near Newbury looking after some ponies.

JOHN COOPER

I was born on 27th October 1928 in Boxtree Cottage, Castle Street, a large farmhouse, gaslight downstairs, candles upstairs.

Castle Street looking north c1936. The Jubilee Oak is still enclosed in wooden paling, having been planted in 1935 to celebrate the Jubilee year of King George V.

Grandfather was a market gardener. My mother was in service at Curtis's on the main road at Murrills Farm and died when I was seven; an aunt brought me up. The market garden stretched from the old *White Hart* which my grandfather owned and ran — it was pulled down in 1938 — on the corner of White Hart Lane up as far as Marina Grove and down to the shore. Most of that was grandfather's market garden. He grew everything. Then we went to the market in Charlotte Street, Portsmouth. We used to leave at 3 o'clock in the morning with horse and cart, and unload. There were two policemen in Portchester. We were very frightened of them. One was called Mr Halls and the other Mr Nice. They both lived in Castle Street, in police houses.

A chap called Horace Woods used to charge batteries up for the radios in those days. My job every Saturday morning was to take up the battery and I think it cost 6d [$2^{1/2}$p]. You got one from there and picked the other one up a week later.

In those days it was all coal fires. The coalman was a Mr Ponting. He came round in a horse and cart until he managed to get a little lorry. We had a bag every week.

We had a teacher called Mr Louwer at Castle Street School. He was a very good teacher with sport. At secondary school I got into sport again where we had a very good teacher, Mr Barker. He managed to get quite a good football team up together. He tried to get me a trial with Bournemouth but I was young and fancy-free.

EDGAR LONG *[born in September 1915]*

My earliest memories — walking along Castle Street on Armistice Day, that was 1918, a procession with all the children waving flags. I was with my sister and a friend.

Father was in the baking business at the end of Castle Street. He had worked in Martell's Nursery which was behind the bakery and was trained as a nurseryman. We had a general shop as well and people came in and bought over the counter, groceries, fresh vegetables, vinegar which had to be measured out into a pint pot. Everything had to be weighed on scales, cheese, butter; even pepper had to be weighed. Some of them paid weekly, some of them paid on the spot. We sold cotton, elastic, needles and pins, everything, pots and pans, brushes. Open 8.00am to about 7 in the evening, six days a week, half day closing on a Wednesday. The shop lasted 'til 1950'ish.

After Castle Street School I went to Mile End House School in Portsmouth for a couple of years then I went into the bakery business. It was the last thing I wanted to do but at that time unemployment was high.

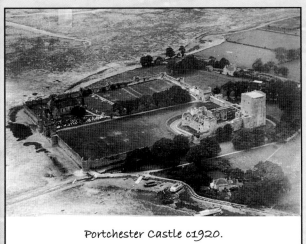
Portchester Castle c1920.

I can remember the walkway outside the Castle being built in 1926. They brought Welsh miners here and a lot of unemployed people and they used them to dig out the inner moats and from that built a sea wall from Hospital Lane right round the Castle. It had a little railway running down from inside the Castle. It was pushed by hand and then pulled back by a horse. They were little trucks like miners' trucks.

MARJORIE MILLER (MADGE) *[was born 5th April 1914 and later lived at 74 Castle Street]*
In the Infants' School the school teachers were Miss Lilly Easton and there was a Mrs Martell, from Lee-on-the-Solent, and she had brothers in Castle Street. There was no gas or electric laid on when mother and father first came to Portchester. They had to manage with oil lamps.

Mother did a bit of mending clothes because the money wasn't much because they didn't get children's allowances then.

My father did the ironwork for the chassis at Hayter's and for lawnmowers and made the iron gates for the Watergate at the Castle.

I had an accident – I chased my brother and ran into this motorbike. I had a fractured femur. There wasn't much work about then – only domestic work and I did that at home. Bread was $2^{1/2}$d [$1^{1/2}$p]. I always worked at home and looked after my parents.

JOHN MEATYARD
I was born in East Street in 1947. We can easily trace our family back six or seven generations, including one George James Meatyard who was a keeper of the prisoners on the old hulks off of Portchester. He's actually mentioned in several books.

Father went by pushbike to Southampton for five years as an apprentice engineer. He left and worked in the one and only general shop in Portchester in the twenties with his parents. It was on the corner of Castle Street right where the NatWest Bank is now. It had an exciting name, it was called 'The Stores'! They sold the shop in about 1935 to what was then the National Provincial Bank when my grandparents retired. My grandfather, Frank George Meatyard – my Dad was Philip George – was a wheelwright by trade and he used to work for what was Hayter's Wheelwright Shop which was roughly opposite the Downsway. In his earlier years he worked for the Leigh & Company Pipe and Putty manufacturers, he was their salesman. He'd go away for up to a fortnight at a time with his horse and cart, selling pipes throughout Hampshire and into Sussex. When he used to run out of stock he would have another load taken by train to the nearest station and off he would go again.

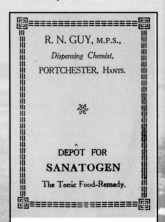

R. N. GUY, M.P.S.,
Dispensing Chemist,
PORTCHESTER, HANTS.

DEPOT FOR
SANATOGEN
The Tonic Food-Remedy.

Guy the Chemist card 1936. Guy's was next door to Meatyard's store at the north end of Castle Street, where the NatWest Bank now stands.

CYNTHIA (MOLLY) BURTON & AILEEN (BETTY) ASH [twins, born on 15th December 1917]

Father was in the Educational Corps in Hilsea and we lived in White Hart Lane while waiting for a house to be built in East Street – 23 East Street. We were then about four or five. We were there for over 30 years in East Street. In the 1930s we rode bicycles to Bognor, Hayling Island, Winchester, Fareham.

We would go for walks over the hill, pick fresh mushrooms and have them for breakfast. It was lovely then. Our parents used to like playing whist in the Parish Hall or the White House Café. We were in the Guides. Mary Ann Sturgess took the Guides. In the 1930s we had odd jobs before the war broke out.

COLIN BARTLETT

I was born 15th October 1923, had two brothers and three sisters and father was a military man. He came from Gloucester to Crown House during the First World War. I was born in Newtown at number 4. It was pulled down for road widening. I went to Castle Street Juniors. There was only one school here then. When I left school I

Castle Street Centre, August 2006. Formerly Castle Street School, it was opened in 1873.

went to The Mount at the top of the hill and was a gardener's boy. I didn't have much idea about gardening but there weren't many jobs around at the time. They never had greenhouses up there at the time [1937], we used to grow the plants from seeds. A lot of it they used to sell down at Fareham Market.

JOHN TAYLOR [very young in 1927]

I was born in Newtown. My paternal grandfather was a Royal Marine and my father had four brothers and a sister and three of those were in the Royal Marines. My father's wages as a foreman gardener in Portsmouth were £2.50 to £3 a week by 1939. My grandfather was employed as the road sweeper for Portchester. His name was George but he was known to everyone in the village as 'Dearoh'. That is in the book 'My Goodness! My Portchester!'. He was never amiss to talking and he listened intently and if it was trouble, his response was always 'Oh dear, oh dear'.

ALAN HEWLETT

I was born in Newtown in 1928 and went to school in Fareham at the Church of England Junior School by St Peter's and St Paul's Church. I used to travel in on the bus. I got a scholarship from there to Price's Grammar School and passed my school certificate and my higher school certificate. I took an examination for Fleetlands Royal Naval Aircraft Repair Yard, as it was then, and passed that and became an Electrical and Radio Fitter Apprentice.

COLIN SELWAY [A very young man in 1927]

We moved from Cosham to 24 White Hart Lane, on the corner of Bayly Avenue, into a brand new bungalow bought for £750 in 1938. Bayly's yard was on the south side of White Hart Lane. Some housing was £475 with a £10 deposit. If you were naval personnel with 21 years' service there was no deposit.

LESLIE NOON [young in the 1930s]

In 1965, bringing legal and financial experience together, I opened the estate agency. Portchester was always a little village which was completely and utterly marred by a factory known as the 'Plucrop Factory'. This was right on the coast and they used to deal with all the waste products of the cattle industry. It had the foulest smell which pervaded the atmosphere right across Portchester. Only on certain days could you avoid it. On Monday mornings, when they first opened up the ovens, the local tradesmen would tell me that they could drive down some roads, and not others, and get this awful whiff. This held back Portchester's development for years!

The source of the 'Portchester Pong'. The Midland Cattle Product factory in the late 1970s.

Most of Portchester on the southern side was built in the 1930s by small local builders, many of whom were financed by solicitors who literally used to put up the money for the builder. The builder of the pre-war era was A J Rogers. He lived in a detached house, which is now The Keep. He sold the site to A G Collins, a Portsmouth builder. One hundred houses have been built where he used to live.

PETER WELLS [born in 1930]
We lived in Leith Avenue in the first bungalow that was ever built on the side of the hill. My father was the foreman builder and he worked for a man called Berney who built all those bungalows. We lived in the first one, two doors away from the *Portsdown Inn*... but the pub wasn't built then. My father's name was Leslie Mafeking Wells. He was born in 1900 on the relief of Mafeking. My brother was a carpenter and he worked on the side of the Hill, building the oil storage tunnels in about 1938/39. My sister was a barmaid in the *Railway Hotel*.

My brother caught diphtheria twice. He had the upper bedroom... and they had to seal the room off. The door was taped around the opening and they placed a candle in the middle of the room to fumigate the room.

JEAN TOONE [very young in the 1940s]
My grandfather came from Southampton in 1896 and he walked to Portchester and found work in the Clay Pipe factory in Castle Street. His name was Henry Baker and he is very well known. His photograph is everywhere you go. In all the museums you will see a photograph of Grandpa Baker.

My father was in the Royal Navy and he was on the Royal Yachts – that was 1919 to 1939. He saw a lot of King George V and Lord Mountbatten.

CHRIS LAVIS
My grandmother's parents were the cook/housekeeper and the coachman at Cams Hall. That was George Fry who married Harriet Lane in 1878, having both been born in 1856. They had come from Cranbourne in Dorset. My mother and her other cousins were invited over at the weekends and then they were fed at a large table in the kitchen.

George Fry was allowed to take the family out in the horse and cart. The family used to visit the *Delme Arms*.

My grandmother, Harriet, went into service in the old Coal Exchange up in London near the Mansion House. The youngest child was Eva and she went into service at Horsham and Eva actually moved back home and looked after her parents in 5 White Hart Lane in 1928 [the home since the 1970s of Paul and Hazel Woodman, Chairman of The Portchester Civic Society.]

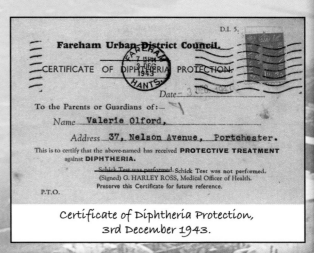

Certificate of Diphtheria Protection, 3rd December 1943.

9

A view from 800 feet of Horsea Island and its Torpedo Testing Range, taken by an RAF pilot flying from Grange Airfield at Gosport on 8th July 1932. A sparsely populated Portchester in the background.

JOAN EASTMAN

I was just two when we moved to Portchester from rented rooms in Portsmouth. The lady was putting up the rent. My father said 'We are just paying money out and not getting any return. They are building all these properties in Portchester so I will go and have a look.' He looked at the Downsway but it had metal windows and the chaps at work said they would corrode because of the salt, go for wooden windows. So he came back on his bike and chose a house with wooden rather than metal windows and where the evening sun is in the back garden. We got No. 17 The Fairway, in about October 1935.

At school the first teacher was Miss Sturgess, of the farm along West Street, then the next class was Miss Winn. The school sometimes was shut – something went wrong with the toilets and we were given a brown envelope to take home and that had cards with maths and English and spelling on and then you filled that in and the following morning you went back again and handed the envelope in.

JOHN TOWSE

When I was a boy in the 1930s we were still paying only 8/- to 10/- a week rent [40p-50p]. I used to go up with the rent to Mrs Gates with the rent book, weekly. Couldn't afford to pay her more than weekly in those days!

ALAN HEWLETT

Father bought a bungalow in the Downsway in 1935 for the handsome sum of £540.

KATHLEEN WELLS

I worked at the glove factory in Havant for years as a machinist.

JOAN MILES

I was born in Cambridge. My father was in the Navy so my mother was almost a single parent as my father went away on two and a half year commissions which were common then. He was based at Chatham and my sister Angela was born while we were there. With war threatening Winston Churchill decided to mobilise the Navy. The Navy was his 'baby' so he looked at all the experienced ratings and did something totally unheard of in the Navy, which was to allow them to move up from the lower deck to the wardroom. We came to Portsmouth – and then Portchester – where HMS *Vernon* was the centre for naval torpedo, gunnery and electrical officers. They all had to work so hard to pass the exams. I know father was up all night as I would get up in the morning to go to school and his head would be on the table asleep over his books. But he passed all his exams and then in 1938 he became a Warrant Officer and carried on to become a Commander during the war.

Aerial view of Portchester Castle c1920.

Portchester IN LIVING MEMORY

Chapter Two –
On Active Service During the War
1939 – 1945

EDGAR LONG

I volunteered straight away and I was called up on the day before war broke out to join the Navy as a Supply Assistant. I served in Portsmouth Barracks for a week then I was drafted to HMS *Suffolk*, a cruiser. We sailed to Scapa Flow and were quite near where the *Royal Oak* was sunk. Then we went down to the Mediterranean, to Alexandria. Later we were sent back up to the Northern Patrol. I have pictures of the *Suffolk* with ice all over the bows. We were up there and we were ordered to bombard Stavanger airfield which we did. We had no escort, only two destroyers, and we were bombed across the North Sea. We managed to struggle back to Scapa Flow and the fleet came out to escort us in. Later I was in Mauritius.

LESLEY PEARCE

In the war I joined the Royal Engineers. Three weeks in the army and over to France! We went through to the French/Belgium border and up towards Brussels. We could see the Germans coming. Then the order came to retreat and it was every man for himself. We got back to Dunkirk and they were bombing every 20 minutes. I walked around Dunkirk for quite a bit, dodging the bombers. I went into a bomb crater, threw my overcoat over me and the bombers went over. Then I went into a building for cover and there was a French medical officer inside. He said 'Good God, you look starved' so I said 'Yes I am.' He brought back a loaf and it was just like eating treacle. Of course that done me alright!

I found the *Queen of the Channel*, a pleasure steamer turned into a hospital ship. I met the commanding officer; I was the first man he met. He wanted to know where the men were, I said they were out in the cellars. He said 'Well what do you want to do, go back on the ship or come with me?' I said 'I'll go with you and call

Portchester's Civil Defence team in 1940.

the men out.' We went along the road, into some woods and met troops to bring them back to the hospital ship. Within ten minutes the ship had started its engines and away we went. At day break the next morning a German bomber dropped a bomb on the ship. It killed the engineer. Another one dropped in the water in front of us; the skipper must have turned the boat just in time. We sent out an SOS and another ship taking petrol and ammunition to Dunkirk came and picked us up. It had got orders to return to England because they wouldn't be able to land it you see. It came and picked us up, pulled away from the ship as it was going down. The skipper said 'Well lads, if we get hit now it will go up like a bomb. This ship is filled with petrol and ammunition'. We saw one of our own planes chasing a German and he shot it down in the water. We were lucky we did not take a hit. The *Queen of the Channel* was sunk.

We got back to Dover where there was a train waiting for us. I was dropped off at Dorset. After about five weeks we got sent to Scotland and ended up at Montrose. I was on telephone duty 24 hours a day. I got a chap to do a shift for me. I said I like a game of whist so I went down in the local town and met my wife.

JOHN TAYLOR

I joined up in 1941. We had a family tradition of Royal Marines. When it came to having to sign the papers there had to be parental permission. My father said 'Are you sure you want to join the Royal Marines?' I said 'Yes Dad' 'I don't think so' said he. 'I do' I said.

I enjoyed my time because a lot of things happened in the 16 years I was in. In 1944 I went to Normandy on HMS *Ramillies*, a 29,000 tonne battleship. I had clear eyesight of the beaches. Beneville is on the coastline, if I had a map here I could show you, I think Deauville is there then I think Benouville was shortly afterwards, there's a lot of 'villes' leading out to Le Havre. There were a number of coastal gun batteries and we had the Beneville one. At 5am we opened fire on them. We heard by about half past six, seven o'clock that we'd destroyed them so we withdrew. In the course of our engagement we'd heard that there were E-boats out because Le Havre was an E-boat – a motor torpedo boat – base. We knew we had anti E-boat patrols, destroyers, out but they also sent out one or two extra destroyers which were inshore bombarding to back them up. One of them was the Norwegian destroyer *Svenner* and it was crossing our bows way ahead of us. All we were doing was leaning on the guardrails as one does when you are doing nothing at all. We were just completing a turn, when suddenly shouts went up amongst the mariners, 'Tin fish'; we didn't call them torpedoes, three coming straight at us from astern. We were completing our turn; they'd been fired when we were port side on and it was just the turn of the ship that meant two went down our port side and one went down the starboard side. We breathed a sigh of relief. We looked forward to see all three went into the destroyer. One minute she was a ship, next minute she was two halves going down, all hands lost. I was only seventeen then.

HMS Ramillies in 1943.

VIC RESTALL

I was in the Territorial Army and I was called up for service on 28th August 1939 and I belonged to the Hampshire Heavy Brigade which was coastal defence. Our wartime billets were the sea forts out on the Solent, Culver Cliff on the Isle of Wight and Bembridge and I served there throughout the war. I instructed Home Guards in gunnery.

RUBY FRANKUM

In 1941 or 1942 women that were not doing war work – I had been working in shops in Commercial Road, Portsmouth – had to

Wren Ruby Frankum, née Hayter, in Trafalgar Square. World War 2.

register and we were conscripted either to go into factories making ammunitions or join the services, so I volunteered to be a Wren. I did my training in Southsea and I was drafted to Whale Island cleaning guns, then I went down as a boat crew Wren. I was a 'mobile' Wren which meant that I had to live in quarters. My brother joined up in 1943 and he was killed in 1944. Then I went down to boats crew and worked as a boat crew Wren and I thoroughly enjoyed it.

JOAN MILES

My father, Alden, was at sea most of the war, he was in Atlantic convoys and the Mediterranean and also terrible Arctic convoys.

BOB NORTH

My Dad was in the Navy and he is from London, same as my mother was. They moved down this way to Marina Grove. It was a new estate, brand new... He joined in 1916. He did 33 years and he came out about 1946-48, finishing his time at HMS *Collingwood*. He was a Master at Arms. Sadly he died quite young, he was only 54.

RON SPARSHOTT

I got called to the services... I was called into the Royal Tank Regiment in 1940 and in 1941 I was in Alamein and then went across to Italy. We were in Churchill tanks with the flame throwers. It was the co-driver who operated them and the flames used to go about 100 yards (92m). When you had used that, the co-driver would just press the button and the trailer containing the flame thrower fuel would be left behind so you went into battle.

Chapter Three –
On the Home Front 1939 – 1945

JOHN TAYLOR
I can recall Sunday the third of September 1939 as though it was yesterday. Just before 11am you were sat down in a chair and you knew you didn't have to speak. You had to listen... to Neville Chamberlain on the wireless. The words I shall never forget. Immediately he finished you could hear on the radio the sirens. Melodramatic I think.

DOROTHY WHITING
Yes, I opened a shop called the Family Stores [in West Street, on the corner of Fairways,] when we came to Portchester in summer 1939. We converted the shop into a grocer's store. Wholesalers were wonderful really because I didn't know anything about retailing and they were so good to me and my Canadian husband.

Dorothy Whiting outside
the Fairway Stores, c1967.

To get their rations each week people used to come and collect them with their ration books and then I used to take little bits [coupons] off and then sent them to the food office in Fareham. Nearly everything was rationed. We did sell soap, but it was very difficult to get. A little packet of Woodbines were about 2d [1p]. I had to cut the bacon up myself with a hand slicer.

Half day was Tuesday. We opened on a Sunday morning. One who helped was Marjorie King in the shop, and one was Rosie Clog. We had an errand boy with a bicycle. There was such a community feeling and people were so nice and it was really lovely and the Portchester people I found so friendly. There were other grocery stores – the Co-op and Pinks. I kept shop until 1967, then sold the business and bought a house close by for £4,000.

JOAN EASTMAN
When war came along we went on ration with Mrs Whiting of the Fairway Stores, 127 West Street, and her husband Freddie, we registered with them as well as the Co-op.

STAN HAYTER
My father was the original Stan Hayter who made motor bodies. I didn't go in the business but went on to the Southern Railway. After working as an office lad at Portchester station I had to move away to get a more senior position. In the Second World War I was at Cosham then Cosham Junction Signal Box.

I was in the Local Volunteers which then changed to the Home Guard. We had a full uniform, helmet, boots, the lot! We had five rounds of ammunition; never used the rifle. My father's family business was bombed.

BARBARA CURTIS
I was in the Land Army. We had two pairs of khaki dungarees, two shirts, one pair of breeches, an overcoat after two years, a hat, a mackintosh and two pairs of socks. Twenty-eight bob a week [£1.40p] and half of that had to go to the person you were living with. I was a milker. At 5.30 in the morning we would get the cows in and finish when you could. In the summer it was 10 o'clock at night. Since 1939 everybody was increasing their milk production.

The Home Guard marching north
up Castle Street. Early 1940s.

BARBARA WATSON

I was born in 1922 and joined the Women's Land Army in 1942, working about seven miles from Winchester. I was in the cowshed milking cows twice a day by machine, but we had to strip them by hand. Red Polls, British Friesians, Jersey, Guernsey. I loved the work.

I joined on my own. There were 20 of us met at Winchester station, high heels, hats on, coming from the town. They sent a dirty old lorry to pick us up. We had half a day a week off but the three other girls in the cowshed were local and they were kind enough to let me have one day off a fortnight, so I had one day's, you know, lay in bed. Me Mum used to bring me breakfast up – and they had to get up seven days a week. I came by train, Eastleigh to Portchester and back, then get a bus from Eastleigh to Hursley.

BETTY ASH

When war broke out, I went to the Pay Corps at Hilsea until it moved to London at the Christmas. Then I left there and went to Vospers, making torpedo boats. I was in the Cardex Department where they priced the thing. And then later I had my son.

We used to queue up at Wheeler's for bread when we knew it was in. Mum used to make bread as well.

Jack, my husband, was wounded at Dunkirk. The night of D Day we saw all the army lorries all go by – wounded soldiers going to Southampton or Netley. Queen Alexandra – that was an army hospital during the war.

COLIN BARTLETT

When the war came, they wanted everyone in munitions in those days so I went to Vospers building motor torpedo boats. There was only one size when I first went there, 70 footers [22m] I think they were. They had American Packard engines I think. One of my sisters was in the ATS in the war.

ELIZABETH POOLE

I took the exam and decided to be a clerical assistant and so I started in the Dockyard just when war was declared. I was 16, yes. It was mainly ledger work, suppliers, material suppliers to the ships. The Southdown 45 bus was 10d to the main gate [4p]. Wages were about £3.

Southdown 45A bus at Southampton Road
bus stop (now Newtown) in 1957.
The 45A went through Portchester via
White Hart Lane and the 45 along the main road.

With rationing we had one egg a week but mother decided it might be better if we kept chickens. She had to buy maize and she used to cook potato peelings and vegetable leavings. I can remember that smell now.

Something similar to parcel tape was criss-crossed across the windows so that if there was any blast it would stop them shattering. There was an anti aircraft gun on the corner of Jubilee Road, it was put there every night. Father was a fire warden to make sure that incendiary bombs hadn't landed on the roof and watching out for things like that.

I got married on the 1st February 1942 in St Mary's Church, and it was cold, it was snowing. Then we caught the coach to Bournemouth for our honeymoon. He was in the Navy on motor launches and they did the Portsmouth to Ramsgate convoy because there were German E-boats in the Channel...

My marriage failed and after five years in London I came back with my daughter.

PHYLLIS WATERMAN *[very young in the late 1920s]*

My first job in 1943 was at a hospital near Petersfield. I thought I would be working with children but I'm afraid I wasn't allowed to be near them. I was a glorified domestic. I had to live in. I had seven bedrooms, 27 stairs and two long corridors and scrubbed down the front of the domestic house too. I had help with cleaning the chapel and help with cleaning the common room and helped serve at table as well.

My next job was in a grocer's. Food came in large amounts, like a block of butter, block of cheese, and 28 lbs [13kg] of sugar, and we had to weigh it. Rationing, even small amounts like 2 oz [about 60gm] of butter; what one person could have. I used to be sent down early in the morning to queue at the Co-op in Portchester for offal.

My next job was at Vollers, the corset makers in Portsmouth, with laces at the back, the studs and whale-bone as well. The machines were twin needle. I was a hook and eye machinist. Hooks and eyes came in strips on a large roll, hooks fixed on one side and eyes on the other of course.

JOHN TOWSE

My father was away in the Navy and so my two sisters, myself and my mother, before the shelters were built, used to huddle in the cupboard under the stairs. We were like that for the first year or so of the war whenever there was a chance of an air-raid. The first Anderson shelter [near us] was built in 120 Castle Street, 1941 or 1942, we could only all huddle together in that one shelter – us four and the people who lived there, the Pratts. The people who lived in this house, 124, were our cousins, Cyril Gates and his mother.

At school I took the old scholarship at 11+. Mr Crocker was the headmaster. First we had to do an intelligence test and if we did well enough in that then we were allowed to take the scholarship for Purbrook Park County High School. To Purbrook was a bit of a traumatic journey because we had to have a bus to Cosham, another bus to the *Hampshire Rose* at Purbrook and then walk all the way down Park Lane. It was grim before we had a school bus at White Hart Lane. We had a fairly wide choice; we could have been to Price's or a school in Petersfield.

Bomb Damage in the Crossway (No. 131 is the house between the bungalows) after the raid on the night of 26/27th April 1944. Three land mines hit Portchester that night, two in the Crossway and one at the north end of Chalky Walk which demolished the blacksmith and Horace Hayter's workshop.

RUBY FRANKUM

My parents' house was bombed, the business went all in one go and some relatives died all on one night, but my parents were okay, but they had nowhere to live. It was in The Crossway. I was on duty in the harbour and saw these aircraft coming over and could see the bombs falling; they got a lot in Portchester, that was in 1944... After our honeymoon my mother and father had found a bungalow that had been badly damaged but we cleaned it up and we all lived together in the Crossways. We slept on the floor because we had no bedding. We literally had nothing.

MADGE MILLER

They used to grow cabbages and carrots and the usual things, potatoes. We had very heavy rain once and the cabbages were washed out. We were bombed when we lived in West Street, next to Hayter's garage and workshops. Father couldn't go back to work again – not there – because it was bombed. We went to Waterlooville for a short time [and came back.]

COLIN SELWAY

I remember a Bofors gun, which is a mobile ack-ack, outside the front door very often. There was a line of barrage balloons right across north Portsmouth Harbour which ran through Portchester. They were roughly a quarter of a mile or so apart and the one at the Castle was shot down while there. They retrieved it. They used to repair them at Titchfield I believe.

A stick of bombs came down Cornaway Lane. There were two or three craters where the *Seagull* is now. They weren't as big as the one in Neville Avenue. It took four houses down I think. People were killed.

I left school and worked at Vospers as an office boy at Crown House. I was the errand boy, the dog's body! I would go and get the cigarettes and the rations from Vospers. The rations were for the office workers. Companies were allowed so much sugar and tea and they rationed it out to the staff and I would distribute it. I used to do the filing at Vospers... I became a corporal in the Army Cadet Corps and I used to go to Newtown where they trained another squad. I went there with Bill Glanville, who owned Glanville's Restaurant at Denmead, and John Thornton. I was in the 14th Hampshire's and then the 17th. I progressed upwards by going to the Tudor Drill Hall at Cosham.

Then I took up painting and decorating some of the war damage! There wasn't any wallpaper then so we used to use distemper and stippled colours on it so it looked like wallpaper! For paint we had quite a lot of linseed oil when we started and some white lead which we used to make the paint. I actually decorated Murrills' farmhouse after the war.

DOROTHY BOXALL [young in the 1930s]

The war was frightening at the time and poor old Mum with all us kids, three of us. Dad had an allotment in those days, we had rabbit, chicken, everything we could use for food.

EDWARD SNELL [brother of Dorothy Boxall]

I went off to hospital and I remember running into the Morrison shelters that doubled up as a table in the ward. I can remember screaming my head off when me Mum used to visit and of course she couldn't come in. Hey, you know, I learnt sign language very quickly in an isolation hospital; at Knowle Hospital.

PETER WELLS

We moved to 9 Grove Avenue. At the end of Grove Avenue was a Barrage Balloon site. That got shot down a couple of times by Germans. We had an air raid shelter in the garden but we couldn't use it because it was full of water. When it was necessary we did occasionally use it ...an incendiary bomb landed on our wall at the front of the bungalow. My mother grabbed a sand bag, went outside and plonked it on the bomb. Down the end of Neville Avenue there was a few shops. Fred Ware had a shop, papers... just outside the shop on the corner was a Smokey Joe, an oil burner. They lit it up when the wind was in the right direction to put the smoke over Portsmouth Harbour... didn't it stink! It used to burn tar or crude oil. It was a great big furnace with a great big chimney at the end. I think there were several in Portchester. My mother worked at Vospers, she was a cook there during the war. When I left the Navy in 1955 she was still working there.

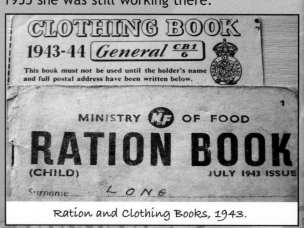

Ration and Clothing Books, 1943.

ROSA BARKER *[Came here in 1939 aged 21 to teach at Portchester Secondary School]*

I taught PE and games, music, biology, English, arithmetic. They were the main subjects. Girls for PE wore their knickers and blouses. Bare-footed I got the girls to go and of course I was in my shorts and blouse and bare-footed. Mr Barker who did the boys, he wore his track suit most of the time because he was Loughborough trained for his PE you see.

There was a lovely atmosphere in the school, partly I think because the war was on and everybody was pulling together. The school couldn't open straight away because they hadn't got the air raid shelters done and even then they didn't have any seating in them or lighting. They were brick-built above ground. All the members of staff were issued with a torch so that when the siren went and we had to go into these shelters we had a torch and we could go round and see that there was no hanky panky going on! The woodwork master had made a stretcher thing so that if there were any accidents, we had one there. We had six boys who were the stretcher party.

We had one or two dogfights up overhead. We had to do fire-watching. Members of staff had to take their turn. Also at the time we had a youth centre running which my husband Arthur was responsible for. When I had my son he was the youngest firewatcher when he was six weeks old. He used to come to school with me in his carrycot!

We were married in 1942 at St Mary's Church at Portchester. He started like I did when the school first opened. Because of Arthur's PE and army cadet work and youth centre work, he did only nine months in the forces then they released him. There were only two people in the whole of Hampshire who were released and he was one of them.

Sports days, which went on all through the war, we had to have down at the Castle. The school remained open in August and as my husband and I were PE people, we put on swimming. We used to take them down to the Castle for swimming. More than once we had dogfights and I'd blow my whistle and off they'd all run and get into the Portchester Keep...

We had the evacuees from Portsmouth come to our school. We would literally feed them. I would have to get up from home, get to school, give them their breakfast, these people, give them a meal in the evening and they would sleep on the school premises. They were supplied with blankets and if they were pregnant they had a mattress! A lot of people who were evacuated to Portchester liked it so much they remained there after the war.

A lot of the children were losing their fathers. You were not only teaching you were also being a kind of person to share their sorrows and sadness with them. There were never any problems, not really anyway, they were so lovely. I loved my teaching.

RUTH MITCHELL *[born in 1935]*

I remember actually seeing the tanks going through Portchester ready for D Day, being stood at the end of Jubilee Road. In Fareham I can remember seeing all the tanks and lorries under the trees around Highland Road area.

My friend, next door, her father was home and he was in the ARP. Sadly he was home because his wife was ill. Only he and one or two other men in the road were left.

Marjorie Bowden enjoys a sunny day outside the Castle, c1940. The wooden building in the background was the Custodian's bungalow, built around 1800 as a guardhouse and demolished in 1962.

Chapter Four – Church Life

JOHN TOWSE

My grandfather (my mother's father) was actually drowned on a Sunday School outing from Portchester in a boat off of Lee-on-Solent pier in 1907. He was in a boat with two of the girls from the village, one of whom was one of our cousins. The girls got up to change places and the boat capsized and he fell out. His name was Staples and they lived at 132 Castle Street.

EDGAR LONG

I was in the Methodist Church when the new vicar came to the parish church, Cyril Spinney. He was quite an active youth worker. I got friendly with him and the other youths and I joined the St Mary's Church then. I was about 17 (that was in 1932) and then I joined the choir. There were three services, the 8 o'clock, the 11 o'clock and the 6.30pm. On Saints' Days they had a service at 8 o'clock in the morning.

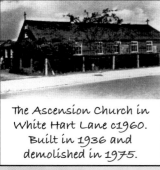

The Ascension Church in White Hart Lane c1960. Built in 1936 and demolished in 1975.

Then money was given for a church at the top of White Hart Lane – which was the Church of the Ascension. It flourished very well until the 1950s.

We were married in 1948 and had our reception in Turret House. That was a big Georgian house that was owned by the church at the time. The curate lived upstairs and downstairs there was a large room that was previously a ballroom where they could hold receptions.

RUBY FRANKUM

We went to the Sunday School of an old church in Castle Street called the Wesleyan Chapel, which was later turned into stables and is now private accommodation. Then the new Methodist Church was built in Castle Street in 1933 on the site of Fig Tree Cottage where an aunt and uncle previously lived. So from early days we have belonged to the Methodist Church. We always went to Sunday School and eventually I was a Sunday School teacher until the war came and then I joined up.

The Methodist Church in Castle Street, August 2006. The church was built in 1933.

My boy friend was in the Fleet Air Arm, he had been abroad for about two and a half years when I just had a letter to say 'See you tomorrow', so we got married the next week, in August 1944. I was nearly 22. We had met when we were fifteen, we were kids really. We were married in the Methodist Church. I borrowed a wedding dress. We had no money. We went up to relatives in the North of Scotland on a train which took 28 hours to get there, war time, packed with troops...

I always belonged to the church and I used to help with the lunch clubs.

RUTH MITCHELL

School classes met in Turret House. It had been bought by the diocese in about 1937 and they had some nuns – I think either Sisters of Nazareth or Bethany – Protestant nuns and they lived at the top of the house. They had what I assume had been built on as a ballroom at one time with a small altar at one end that they could shut off. The house had shutters. I went to Sunday School there for a while. My mother had a great friend called Mrs Trotter who was a caretaker there almost up to the time they pulled it down. Turret House was a big building built in about 1740. It had a turret at the top. I think the turret was so that signals could be relayed to the Castle via St. Vincent House in Castle Street. Castle Street School also had two classrooms, I assume rented, in the Methodist Church, and I had a year out because I had to go to a sanatorium for a year.

West Street, Portchester looking east, c1960. Turret House on the left and the present Noon's Estate Agents jutting out on the right.

JEAN TOONE
I went to school in the 1940s in Turret House for a year. It was a lovely, lovely old house, lovely grounds and trees. Then to Manor House, it was a new school in the 1940s when I was six. I was married at 17, and a mother at 18 with a son and daughter.

JIM ERSKINE
I started to play football for the Life Boys and the Boys' Brigade before 1938 and we arrived at Portchester in 1952. We became members of the church. The Reverend Cardale was there at the time and he was a team cricketer and rugby player. He used to come and watch us play football.
My wife helped with the Sunday School at the Ascension Church in White Hart Lane and she went there and I ended up a sidesman.

VIC RESTALL
We have never drunk. We are tee-totallers and as Salvationists that was part of our agreement, not that we actually wanted to drink.

MOLLY BURTON & BETTY ASH
We used to sing in the choir at St Mary's. We knew Edgar Long and his wife Mabel. We used to go to the Isle of Wight and the New Forest for an outing occasionally. Our brother, George Salisbury, who was killed, used to be a Server at the church. He has got a plaque in the Fareham Council Offices and they took it up to the [new] offices.

PETER WELLS
I was a bit of a churchgoer in those days. Reverend Spinney was our vicar and he was a really nice old man. We belonged to the Boys' Church Brigade and we had a little uniform with a cap. We used to have sports days down there which he used to organise. I was a choirboy in St Mary's and was confirmed there as well. I remember you used to get 2s.6d. [$12\frac{1}{2}$p] for a wedding and 2/- [10p] for a funeral. Sometimes they were looking for someone to go round the back and pump the organ. We would sit reading a comic and the sound would go wrong and we would think 'Oh God, better get on it again.' You had to keep the lead weight at the top of the box by pumping it so that the organist had plenty of air to play with. I quite liked the church down there.

St. Mary's Church, August 2006.

ROSA BARKER
My husband Arthur's job was to go round the whole of Portchester finding houses that could take people that had been bombed out in Portsmouth. One of the people, the vicar, Rev.

Spinney, who married us had this lovely big manse. Only him and his housekeeper were there (she did have children) but he didn't want to take in evacuees. Arthur said 'I'm afraid you are going to.'

NELL WYCHERLEY, MBE [very young in the 1930s]

I became very much part of St Mary's Fellowship since 1979 when we moved here from London. We are a Church of England Church in the Portsmouth Diocese. Originally I came from Barbados and arrived here in London in 1963, having come from Rome. I had been in Italy for a year, singing, and prior to that I was in New York for a year and prior to that I was in South America.

I subsequently became a lay minister. You have to be selected by the Parochial Church Council and a minuted approval had to go before the selection board as well as all the referees and so on. It was three years' training. I am a licensed reader in the Diocese of Portsmouth, licensed at the Cathedral by the Bishop in 1998. It involves preaching and teaching and officiating at funerals both in St Mary's and at the Crematorium. I have had that privilege four times this week so far.

It is a continuing commitment to ministry and pastoral care and is not paid.

At the age of 70, and I have reached that age, you then have 'permission to officiate' with the agreement of the Bishop and the Vicar, renewed every year. I think that the gifts that you have for performing are very helpful in relating and communicating with other people in whatever form of work you are doing. I think that has helped in preaching for instance; it is more than just singing operatics and doing a concert because it is deeper than that...

I don't sing in any professional capacity any more, but I will sing whenever I am asked to. I tend to draw on the repertoire that I have but I am always prepared to learn something new.

MARJORIE (MADGE) MILLER

I went to Sunday School at the Methodist Church in Castle Street with the Reverend Notts and the Reverend Mason. We lived at No 74 Castle Street, on the corner of Cow Lane. Merle Sturgess was my Sunday School teacher – that is Clem's sister. Sometimes we went on trips... and they had what they called dodgems. We went to the Isle of Wight, we looked forward to that, it was a treat. My parents went to church in the evening and one of my aunts came to look after me while they went to church.

RUBY PLOWMAN

Howard Saunders, who ran the Woodcraft Chivalry (a bit like Scouts and Guides, but was boys and girls together) was quite innovative in games and things that he would organise for the youngsters. Winter nights when it was dry but cold we often used to go off in the dark, tracking over the Hill. It amazes me now that we could do that... The Woodcraft Chivalry was an extremely well run organisation and it was held at the Methodist Church. It was

Woodcraft Chivalry parade past Crown House and the Jubilee Oak, c1955.

probably more prominent in Portchester then than the Guides and Scouts. I think because it was mixed. We used to camp out at Liss and we used to borrow a lorry from the farm in Upper Cornaway Lane. We would all pile into the back of the lorry... health and safety didn't really come into it! We used to hire the tents off the Army in Hilsea Barracks. All the cooking pots and things were stored in the old Vicarage. It would have been about 1948/49. Later, children's aims and ambitions changed. They wanted holidays in Spain! So it all died because the expectations of children were so much greater than camping and sitting round a camp fire.

JOAN EASTMAN
A friend was in the British Order of Woodcraft Chivalry at the Methodist Church with Howard Saunders. He got thrown out of the Scouts because he was a conscientious objector. He started the Lodge of the Shining Way and the Reverend was the Reverend Nott. I became a Woodling, I became a Tracker and then when I was older I became a Pathfinder. I used to go to their Moot meeting at Sandyballs Estate down in the New Forest. We also camped at Greatham Mill and had a lovely time. I was Assistant Quartermaster.

If you were Church of England you went along to Turret House and the deaconesses lived there at the back of the house. The other church was the Church of the Ascension, along White Hart Lane, people would go there for services and concerts and plays. One of the shining lights at that time was Miss Betty Balfour-Smith and her mother, they used to live in The Crossway at 'Jonquil' – she used to have the dancing class at her house in the lounge. You would dance and sing and concerts were put on in the Ascension Church Hall and at the Parish Hall

JOHN TOWSE
I was in St Mary's Church choir. There were adult members of the choir who stood behind us trying to keep an eye on the choirboys in the front. There seemed to be about ten small boys, behind would be the elders including Mr Long. Reverend Spinney was the vicar; always used to ride about on his bicycle.

Portchester Lodge of the Shining Way of the Order of Woodcraft Chivalry parade in the Castle.
Probably Remembrance Sunday 1952.

Vicar and Mayor's Chaplain, the Reverend Michael Thomas, greets visitors at St Mary's on the inauguration of Councillor Roger Price as Mayor of Fareham in 1981.

JEAN TOONE

In 1989 Reverend Michael Thomas, the Vicar, asked if we would be involved in a voluntary care group in Portchester to care for those we transport to hospital etc., and the group was set up. It was small, very small at the beginning, but now it has grown and we now have 16 drivers. They go to Southampton Hospital, Haslar Hospital, Gosport War Memorial, St Mary's, Q.A. and BUPA, taking the elderly to the doctors, dentists and opticians. They stay with them and look after them. We also take the elderly to visit their relatives and collect them after a couple of hours. I co-ordinate and have a couple of ladies who help me. Hampshire Social Services helps and the local Health Authorities.

HAZEL WOODMAN

We got involved in the Church, my Nan used to go to the Church a lot. We went to the Ascension Church, which was in White Hart Lane. That was a wooden hut. It was the sister Church of St Mary's down in the Castle. We were very proud of our hut. I got quite involved, not so much with the religious aspect, more with the social side of it. There was a gang of girls that all got together and we all went into the choir as a group. Then we all did Sunday School teaching there. We then got involved with the Galas. When I was between 12 and 15 [late 1950s] the Church took over the running of the Gala when I think Reverend Cardale was the vicar.

In 1971 I married Paul Woodman in St Mary's Church in the Castle. It was absolutely wonderful. We got married on a Wednesday afternoon because the shops closed on a Wednesday afternoon and most of my friends worked in shops. We had a small wedding and had the reception in my home in Kent Grove.

Hazel Bowden (later Woodman) teaching Sunday School in the Ascension Church, c1962.

Chapter Five –
Earliest Memories of the Sporting Life

JIM ERSKINE

I was born in Belfast on 23rd December 1924. I was picked to play for the Irish schoolboys national team in 1938/39. We moved to Portchester in 1952 to a council house allocated to the Admiralty.

I was going to play for Fareham and I couldn't find Fareham football ground so I went to Portchester and stayed with Portchester. We played in the Castle and the changing rooms – there were two places for the changing rooms – over the top of the main entrance and at the far end of the Castle and sometimes we changed there.

Fareham Town wanted me to play for them but I refused to go. We played in the Portsmouth League. We were very good, we played in the Castle and people came and watched us and it was very good. I only see the goalkeeper these days. That was Taffy Jones, he was an ambulance driver and my wife had a car accident and Taffy took her to hospital in the ambulance... I was 40 when I packed up, so that would be 1964.

MOLLY BURTON & BETTY ASH

We went to Harrison Road School in 1928 and played netball in the school team. We played tennis and cricket for Portchester Ladies Club at the Castle. We used to play Horsea Island... underarm bowling.

Portchester Youth Club Football Team. 1945/46 season. Secondary school teacher, Ali Barker on the right, in glasses.

LESLIE NOON

The local bank manager, Bill Wiseman, who managed the National Westminster Bank on the corner of Castle Street, was the local scorer/umpire for the local cricket team on a weekend. The matches took place on the Castle Field. It was a great community spirit.

Football and Cricket Club dinner, c1948.

JOHN COOPER

At secondary school we had a very good teacher, Mr Barker. He was a Yorkshire man and a cross-country runner. He managed to get quite a good team up together in the school and he had contacts everywhere. We had a cricket team and we used to travel round to different schools and play matches.

When I left secondary school I played in goal for Portchester's main team for about nine years. The pitch was in the Castle grounds, much to the disgust of the Ministry of Public Works. They wanted us off.

They played cricket in the summer. We had some jolly good games down there. Eventually they developed a site at Wicor and over time we played our home games there... One of our chaps went into a tackle and his knee just split right open because of flints. The flints work up through the earth. They shut the ground until they cleared the flints.

DOROTHY BOXALL

I played hockey for Portchester School and also for the netball team. I was head girl and the head teacher was Mr Harman. He caned boys and girls, he was a swisher!

ALAN HEWLETT

My father was a keen cyclist and member of the local Cycle Touring Club and was their treasurer for a long time. Eventually I decided I wanted to have a go at something competitive so I took up time trialling with the Hampshire Road Club. We started off at 10 miles but the real time trialling really started when you were doing 25 miles, 30, 50 and 100 miles and then 12 hours. Some of them did 24 hours, 12 hours was enough for me.

My best in 12 hours was 231 miles on a Claude Butler bike. Nowadays they do 260-270 in 12 hours, the roads are better, the equipment is better, the fitness levels are better...

I won the Hampshire Road Best All Round Championship in 1948 and 1949. Strangely I went for a walk down Castle Street and got to a little house alongside the *Cormorant* and a man came out of his door and I said to him 'Have you lived here long?' 'Yes'. 'Good Heavens, you must have known Ray Tacket'.' I *am* Ray Tacket!' he said; 'You used to cycle with the Hampshire Road Club'. 'I did' he said. 'I am Alan Hewlett'.

JOHN MEATYARD

In the late '60s I met my wife through my motor racing days. The nearest chap to me who did stock car racing was George Matthews and through him I met his sister so here endeth that story.

We'd several circuits we used to race stock cars in; nearest one being Southampton.

Portchester Secondary School Girls' Hockey Team, Winter 1957/58.

Ringwood was quite a good circuit. Raced at Eastbourne and Wimbledon a couple of times but yeah, thoroughly enjoyed that.

JOHN TOWSE

Just after the war things were reforming and Commander Hammond and the team reformed the Sailing Club and we all became junior members. The Portchester Ducks was the one the Commander had designed.

The Sailing Club foreshore, c1962. Radio masts on Horsea Island can be seen in the background.

JOHN OAKEY

As a family we joined the sailing club in 1956. That started off as a small compound alongside the clubhouse. A landing craft was the original clubhouse, pulled up on the shore. The property down there came up for sale and we had help from Fareham Council with a loan and Geoff Rushin in the village was competent to know how good the property was. He was a lot of help to establish it. The Council eventually let us buy a bit so we got the freehold of the whole area. Now we have got 800 odd members, all sorts of people.

We were going to give opportunities to young people, all sorts of people. Our Scouts have their moorings and keep their canoes and boats there. This is part of the conditions of one of the loans we had.

Chapter Six –
Post War Portchester
1945 – 1975

RUBY FRANKUM

I had my first child in 1945. I was still living with my mother. I think it was in the 1950s my husband came out of the Navy after he had done seven years special service, but during that time the Korean War broke out and he was called back in. He got a draft to Singapore and I had to follow with two school age children. It took three weeks on a troopship through the Med, Suez. He had found some accommodation so we were a family again. We were there for two years. Then there were a lot of disturbances going on in Malaya and the Chinese were fighting for their independence. We were under armed guard and had to go at 3 o'clock in the morning. We got a draft to fly home and we hopped from Singapore to Bangkok, to Calcutta, to Karachi, to the Persian Gulf, to Cyprus, to Rome and home. Three days flying on a four engined Bristol Britannia. We came back to Portchester in 1955. I was widowed in 1966. He had had malaria several times and it left him vulnerable. He collapsed one weekend and died the next. He was 39...

I had to do something with my life, my children had grown up. So I decided to go to College and I did a three year course at Highbury Technical College on crafts and I did a teacher's course. I could do part-time teaching on crafts. Upholstery was my thing. I taught at Harrison Road, then at Wickham Road, then evening classes in Portchester, Gosport and Southsea. I was going all over the place. It was all adults.

JOHN TAYLOR

The Thicket, well, that stretch of ground to the railway line, before the houses were built, was a German prisoner of war camp. One of my sisters and her friend were walking along the road one day, 1946 or '47 and they met two prisoners walking towards them. They were allowed out. Now one of them, and I still meet him now, was educated in Hanover and went to university so he spoke very good English and stopped and spoke to them. It was years after they got married; I think it was 1968 that Eric and sister Irene went back to Germany and Irene still lives in Germany. Eric died three or four years ago.

DOROTHY WILDING

I started playing bridge when I was 23 and I've only just finished [aged 96!]. I was a founder member of Portchester Bridge Club. We played matches away, to Southampton.

JOHN TOWSE *[a schoolboy in the 1940s]*

The way of getting into the Castle grounds when the tide was down for us small boys was to go through the small tunnel that leads from the outside moat to the inside moat. The Castle was a great source for us to play in. The other great source of amusement to us was to play what was then and still referred to as 'round the banks'. Now, 'round the banks' is fairly obvious really, the banks that run from where is now Vospers to the Castle.

My first job ever which I got paid for was with farmer Stride in Wicor Park. He always employed village boys for potato picking. We had to start at 6 in the morning until 6 o'clock at night for 16/- a week [80p].

Up until 1951 in this terrace, we only had gas lighting. When I was a boy we had no main drainage. We had a large bucket that had to be buried at the bottom of the garden every so often.

The locomotive 'Flying Scotsman' stops at Portchester Station on a railtour, 7th September 1966.

Lansdown Avenue c1960. Many of the roads around Portchester were not made up and tarmacked until the 1960s.

Lansdown Avenue in August 2006.

VERA & RON SPARSHOTT

RON I have been here since 1946 at 47 Hill Road. When you are standing in the garden you can see all the boats coming in and out from France and from the Isle of Wight. People ask me if I am going to move. I tell them that the hill is getting harder, it is not getting flatter! I tell them that I like my view! I went into the Dockyard until 1940, in the service until 1946, and I went back to the Dockyard until I was 60. We married in 1947.

VERA Behind us were two big farms stretching to where the Crematorium is. One was owned by Owen Sturgess. There was also Myra Sturgess, she never married. Clem Sturgess used to live in Leith Avenue. He built quite a lot round here. Lewis sold his little market garden, he built the other side of Portsview Avenue, then he built Kelvin Grove. I used to work over there, picking strawberries for 2d [1p] a punnet. Each punnet weighed about half a pound [227 gm]. They used to grow strawberries, raspberries, cabbages, sprouts, runner beans, etc. for the local market. They used to take the things down to Portsmouth. I think they took it by lorry. There was also Dore Farm and we didn't have a Crematorium then. We lost 8ft [2.5m] of the front garden when they widened the road and put the pavement in.

ALAN HEWLETT

I joined Fleetlands in the late 1940s and I wanted to get into the drawing office, yes, I was mad keen on machine drawing but I couldn't get in. I then took the Admiralty draughtsman's exam and applied for a job and got it at Portsmouth Aviation. After a few months I found that I had passed, but in front of all the other draughtsmen at Fleetlands! I went to the old Technical College in Portsmouth for my ordinary National Certificate then went on to the Higher National. I progressed from Design Engineer to Trials Engineer, testing the equipment made at Portsmouth Aviation for the MOD and I had to go all over the country to establishments approved by the MOD. I travelled the country staying in very nice hotels for some 20 years. My first car was a Consul Convertible Phase 2, in 1957 and I had two Alfa Romeos in succession. I was 'King' of The Downsway!

JOHN COOPER

Towards the end of the war my first job was at a shipyard in Wicor, taken on as apprentice shipwright. Rogers, the builder, was building the shipyard and we helped. We were building motor fishing vessels about 90 ft [28m] long, all wood, which the Navy used for stores and liberty boats. We never had enough deep water to launch them. The first one that was launched went about 40 yards [37m] offshore and got stuck. We had to have a Dockyard tug to pull it out of the creek. We went on to make second wave landing craft for the invasion [of Europe in June 1944]. They were flat bottomed with an 8 Packard engine inside, about 30 ft long [9m] and about 5ft wide [1.6m]. The shipyard did not last very long. Later I worked for Steve Goldring, building houses and bungalows all over the place for years.

In about 1953 the 'big boys' started to buy all the land up. The small builder couldn't compete. I then worked at HMS *Collingwood* for 20 years until I retired. Mr Wellstead, who was secretary of Portsmouth Football Club, got me that job when I was working on my own.

VIC RESTALL

In 1957 George Snocken, Sid Hickiss, myself and Barbara Pratt got together outside the allotments where what is now Shrubbery Close and decided we would like to form the Portchester Allotment Association. We had a chat and the landlord of the *Wicor Mill* pub let us go in to the lounge and we sat in there and discussed things. We passed the note round the neighbourhood. They elected me as Chairman and Miss Pratt as the Secretary cum Treasurer. We held our first show a couple of years later in Stride's field that ran from Cornaway Lane almost to Fareham on the left hand side of the road facing Portsdown Hill. We held that show under canvas; we showed rabbits and vegetables and flowers.

MALCOLM COOPER [very young in 1939]

When we came to Portchester in 1945 I went to Wicor Infants and Junior School. The headmaster was Mr Hargreaves, the deputy was Mr Pearce and a Mr Gerald Durrant was there. The first teacher I remember there was a Miss Paterson.

It was a lot more open and around Shrubbery Close there were allotments. In Marina Grove our house deeds showed Reverend Allcot owned the land and our neighbour Mr Dove used to work for Warings. They levelled the site and he drove the bulldozer and he used to make breeze blocks. He was paid the princely sum of 6d [2½p] per hundred!

At secondary school I passed the written exam for the Dockyard. As an apprentice my first week's pay was £2.1s 4d. [£2.07p].

From 1953 to 1957 I was a scout and achieved the Queen's Scout award and from 1957 to 1997 [I was actively concerned with] the whole programme of teaching and instructing the boys. The test work they had to do was, I

think, a bit before its time because they had to do work on conservation, to recognise trees, birds and things like that. We did training camp for boys who had joined, since the last camp in the summer would be in the Whitsun over at Ashley Down Copse over the back of the hill by Nelson's monument.

The Mayor of Fareham, Councillor Peggy Gardner, reviews the Portchester Sea Scouts on the opening of the Shopping Precinct in 1975.

In the summer we used to try and get near water because we could take the boats and canoes with us and each group of boys would set off for a 24 hour trip in the boats. You had to swim 50 metres before you could ever go out in a boat. Twice we took boys over to the Belgium camp on a site along the River Meuse. There used to be regattas, one at Alverstoke and another at Marchwood, Southampton.

There were no such things as sleeping bags; you had two blankets and half a dozen blankets pins.

For the Sea Scout branch we would have three 'watches' and about 30 boys per watch; then there were three cub packs and a normal scout troop, in excess of 200 boys. We sent boys to jamborees to Greece, Canada. I attended one in 1957 at Sutton Coldfield which was the 50th anniversary of scouting.

JIM ERSKINE

My boy Derek joined the Cubs... They were looking for someone to look after the Scout equipment and my wife volunteered for me to go as quartermaster. We met in Noel Cottage in Castle Street. Commander Cobham had a den on the end of his house and the Scouts met there... I ended up being Assistant Scout Master and I will always remember taking the boys to the Jamboree at Sutton Coldfield. It must have been about 1956 and we took these boys on the train to Waterloo Station and Commander Cobham drove his car up with some of the boys to bring the gear up. We had to put their gear in a taxi with one of the boys and take the gear across London and we got on another train up to Birmingham.

BOB NORTH

One of our teachers was Miss Boxall, she was a very strict lady. She used to throw bits of chalk at you, a dig on the shoulder or rap you across the knuckles with the ruler. I remember going to that school during 1947, it was a bad winter, the snow was piled up six to eight feet in the hedgerows and when we got to school all the milk was frozen. Every classroom had a coke stove at the end of the room, with little railings round it. I was with Mr Grenville, he was my teacher. I had him all the way through...

Portchester Secondary School Teachers, c1959.

An employment advisor came round and I said I wanted to build boats. He said it was a dying trade. He completely put me off. I ended up cleaning windows for Mr Ridgely in Somers Road, Portsmouth. I used to get £6 a week so as a young chap I was well in. I used to cycle from Portchester to Somers Road every day.

We used the pubs a lot, I started going to pubs at about 17 I suppose.

The old Plucrop factory used to stink all the time. It was a terrible smell. It used to get impregnated in the clothes of my mates' dads who worked there.

RON SPARSHOTT

I went back into the Dockyard until I was 60 [1978.] I used to go by train, the 6.30am from the bottom of the road. When they started bringing the buses up this area it was better because the bus used to stop right outside the Dockyard at the Unicorn Gate.

JOAN EASTMAN

My first job at 14 was in the cold winter of 1948 at Charlie Hubbard's, a fish merchant and they had a shop at the Fratton end of Arundel Street. It was a 7.30am start, 5.30pm finish. The job to do in the morning was to go in and the butler's sink would be full of cod cutlets and I had to arrange the cod cutlets on white trays and I worked in the shop. There wasn't a lot of meat so people used to buy a lot of fish. It was one shilling and two and a half pennies per pound [6p for 227gm] for best cod fillet. I got 28/- a week [£1.40p] and I gave my mother 10/-. 10/- [50p] went to the bank and with the other 8/- [40p] I had to get to work. Woodbines were about 5d a packet [$2^{1/2}$p].

RUTH MITCHELL

When I left school... my mother had become a widow and there was a knock at the door one day. It was the owner of a shop in West Street; he had a radio shop and he said "Do you want a job?" That was called Kenneth R Barker's.

People used to come in with accumulators and I was at the cash till. I don't remember seeing much of the boss – I think he nipped off to the Working Men's Club rather a lot!

JOYCE OAKEY [very young in the 1920s]

We came down for a holiday and John went round all the firms and decided to go to Vosper's. I came down on a milk train from Chatham and found a furnished flat, went

Woodcraft Chivalry members march through the Lych-gate to St. Mary's Church for the Armistice Day Service.

shelves in it and it became storage.

I did eventually go to work when the youngest boy was 14. I was Secretary at the Community Centre in Southsea for about 13 years and I became Secretary to the Conservative Agent in Southsea which I found a very interesting job.

JOAN MILES

I was in the post war Wrens so we had a very quiet time compared to my father. We moved to HMS *Mercury* at Clanfield and mother had been at Portchester since 1937. Father died in 1993 aged 89 and they named the hall [at the Community Centre] after him – Alden Hall.

BETTY ASH

I have been in the Townswomen's Guild for over 50 years. They meet in the Methodist Hall now; it used to be in the Parish Hall. I used to be in the Country Dance Section and we used to go out and dance quite a lot.

Castle Street. 2005.

back home and we moved in to the furnished flat with our little boy in August 1955. Our eldest son became a Cub [in the 1950s] with the 3rd Portchester. I became a Cub leader. Molly Cobham was a very persuasive lady and she liked to see us all in uniform. I was a Cub leader until my oldest grandson was about 4 years old and he is now 23. The Cubs became Sea Scouts so they went in John's boat to see Alec Rose come in and we did get photographed down there by somebody. We saw the print in a public house, recognised it as ourselves, and went along and got a copy for ourselves...

I was one of those housewives who didn't go to work and they will be even more rare in the future because we didn't believe in keeping up with the Joneses. If we wanted something, we saved up for it. I did the odd bit of dressmaking for my friends and that gave me my pocket money, but we enjoyed life, we enjoyed our children. I don't like this idea that the children can go to school 'til 6 o'clock in the evening.

We did loads of things with our children and we didn't have a car. We wanted to go camping but we didn't have a lot of money so John made a barrow that was on two bicycle wheels and we took it by train down to the New Forest. We also went by train and went along the Thames and over to the Isle of Wight. On the trains they had a guard's van where you could put the barrow in. When we acquired a Hillman Imp I made a box that was part of the tent system, we stood it vertically and put

BARBARA WATSON

I was born in the old thatched cottage in Castle Street in 1922, my granny's old house. It was burnt down 53 years ago. They've restored it, but it's different. When I came from the Land Army, I worked in the Portchester Post Office in Castle Street. I also worked for Fred Ware who had a little shop at number 3, I think, Castle Street. It sold wool and sweets, toys, it was very nice. I worked there until Les and I married. My granny's shop was the next one to Long's bakery, past the lane, on the right as you come up Castle Street.

We had three sons and have eight grandchildren and they're all living in Portchester. I worked in the *White Hart* when my youngest boy was three. Mum used to have him. I would work in there five days a week, Monday to Friday. We didn't do food then. You could get crisps and that sort of thing but no food. We had no holidays but we did have a car...

HAZEL WOODMAN [very young in the1940s]

I remember when we had an explosion at Bedenham. That was quite a big thing. It was a beautiful sunny evening, early evening I remember. [14th July 1950, 6.47pm, first explosion; 7.15pm, second explosion.] The men were so protective and we all had to go down to where the old air raid shelters were at the bottom of the garden. We sat down in the shelter for quite a while. When we were told we could come out I saw that Mum had these big long pink knickers hanging on the washing line. They were covered in spots of oil! There were all sorts of other bits coming down like burnt paper. We also had problems with the windows' metal frames; we could never open some of the windows after that.

We had a very family oriented life in Kent Grove. I had a special Uncle that used to live next door. When he came home from work we used to play games a lot in the garden with him and my sister Judy, who is 4 years older than me. We played cricket or rounders until it got dark most nights. Our roads were not made up then, all potholes and that. We had a rope that went across the road and we did skipping. We would do that for a long time, maybe stopping every hour if a car went past. There weren't the cars then.

The Gala at that time became enormous. It was even much bigger than it is today. It used to go on way into the evening. We used to decorate floats with the Sunday School children. I think we won 1st prize a couple of times, which was quite nice for the children.

In my thirteenth year my first Saturday jobs were in florists in Fareham and then in Cosham. I then got a job in Carlisles at North End. They had five shops in Portsmouth.

Clothes! I have always been the same. I used to buy Mary Quant shoes in a shop across the road in North End. A hairdresser's a couple of doors away, Andre's, started to sell all the Mary Quant big plastic earrings. I used to start my outfit from a pair of earrings and then I would go and buy the material and make my own clothes.

When we were buying our house we had a very good friend in Mr Noon, the estate agent down in the village. He would say 'I'm going to show you this bungalow today, you won't like it but I've got to show you!' In the end he phoned 'I've got just the place for both of you, it's derelict but you are going to love it'. The house was 5 White Hart Lane where we still are today. It cost us £7,750 in 1971 and it was such a tight squeeze to get a mortgage.

At the top of Marina Grove there was a little shop called Sutcliff's. It was a little sweet shop with jars of all sorts of sweets like liquorice allsorts, barley sugar, Pontefract Cakes, sweet cigarettes and sherbet dabs. He used to open the shop on Christmas Day at 4 o'clock for half an hour to sell ice-cream for your tea. This was before we had a freezer in the house, mid to late 1950s. You had to pay for it beforehand and you had a ticket with your name on. You queued outside waiting for the shop to open and when you went in he

PROGRAMME OF EVENTS

PATRONS

Admiral of the Fleet Sir Algernon Willis, G.C.B., K.B.E., D.S.O.   The Right Reverend The Lord Bishop of Portsmouth

The Fancy Dress Parade will form up at the Cormorant Inn, Castle Street, and March to the Arena where it will be joined by the Guard and Band and Ceremonial Trumpeters of the Worthing Unit, Sea Cadet Corps, all being in position by 1.55 p.m. ready to receive Admiral of the Fleet Sir A. Willis at 2 p.m.   After the inspection of the Guard and Band the Fete will be declared open and the judging of the Fancy Dress Parade will take place.

Part 1		Part 2	
2.30 p.m.	COUNTRY DANCING *by the Girls of Portchester County Secondary School*	MARCHING AND PLAYING *By the Band of the Worthing Unit Sea Cadet Corps*	4.50 p.m
2.50 p.m.	SMALL ARMS DRILL *by the Worthing Unit Sea Cadet Corps*	DANCING DISPLAY *By the Girl Cadets, H.M.S. Victory*	5.0 p.m

SPECIAL ATTRACTION

3.0 p.m. to 3.45 p.m.	**THE DAGENHAM GIRL PIPERS** WHO WILL GIVE TWO SEPARATE PERFORMANCES	5.15 p.m. to 6.0 p.m.

3.45 p.m.	CUTLASS AND HORNPIPE DISPLAY *By the Cadet Corps, H.M.S. Excellent*	PHYSICAL TRAINING DISPLAY *By the Girls of Portchester Youth Centre*	6.0 p.m.
4.0 p.m.	TEA INTERVAL	GRAND FINALE *Sunset Ceremony and March Past*	6.15 p.m

Fareham Red Cross Military Band will be in attendance throughout the afternoon and will play a selection of Music during the Tea Interval.

SHORT EVENSONG IN THE CHURCH—Preacher THE LORD BISHOP   7 p.m. - 7.15 p.m

DANCING IN THE KEEP — 7.30 p.m. to 9 p.m.
Entrance by Ticket — On Sale in the Grounds

Portchester Fete Programme for 1951.
Dancing in the Keep in the evening!

opened the freezer and he had ice cream cut into blocks which he would wrap up. We didn't have ice-cream very often. It was almost as good as opening the presents on Christmas morning! The shop changed hands over the years and is now part of Acorn Vets. On the other side of Chalky Walk was a shop called the Sweet Spot. Every now and again Smiths Crisps used to bag up all their odds and ends and sell them for a penny a bag. Word got around like wildfire (we were at the Secondary School then) as soon as the Sweet Spot had those penny bags. We used to have to queue up as everybody wanted them. They were greasy and full of calories and absolutely wonderful!

An aerial view, late 1960s. From front, Smiths Crisps factory, the A27, Bert's Café, now Mother Kelly's, and Vospers shipyard. Portchester Castle is in the distance.

I can remember the library up Chalky Walk. Mum used to read a lot and as she didn't go out I would go in there with her list of books... Another shop was the Co-op on the corner of Gladstone Gardens. We used to have our groceries delivered once a week and we had a Co-op dividend number but I can't remember it now. There was also in White Hart Lane a newsagent; Mr and Mrs Ware owned that. Ware's also had a tiny little shop in Castle Street that was purely children's clothes. In White Hart Lane you could do all your shopping from vegetables to pharmacy to meat, all sorts of things. We didn't have to go down to the village really; it was all in White Hart Lane.

LESLIE NOON

Houses with garages were rarely demanded in those days. It wasn't until the 1960s that the roads were made up, for example White Hart Lane and the surrounding areas. In the early post war the local builder was Clem Sturgess. He built many houses on the hill slopes. Later on in Laverock Lea and the like, houses with their own drives that he built were very much in demand.

An ammunition barge, moored at Bedenham in Gosport, exploded. I have actually met the people that were involved with it at the time who said, but for the tide being out at the time, it would have demolished half of Portsmouth and half of Portchester. So the local council forbade building in a sort of circle drawn round the area of Hatherley Crescent and Quintrell Avenue and all those fields were never developed.

I remember calling on tenants paying 30/- [£1.50] a week rent and found they could not come to terms and see why they should buy. Many of the residents of Portchester were families who had lived in Portchester all their lives. They used to move from one road to another.

Building societies in that era like the Alliance, the Abbey National, the Halifax and the Portman only had funds that they derived from depositors. That very much governed how much they could lend. By lending three times income, it governed the price of houses. We did not take into account the female's income.

JOHN MEATYARD

I was born in East Street in 1947. My parents had just come back from the war years in Wales. My father started to resurrect his taxi business which he'd left through the war years when he was in the fire brigade. He branched out into coaches.

I started as a motor mechanic at the age of fifteen including a day release at Highbury College, then, when I was 18, I started driving taxis for my Dad until he retired in 1967/68. Taxi work expanded, it was mainly long distance work, airports, London docks and much further afield including doing tour work, seven or ten day or fortnight tours which was quite unusual in those days to places like Scotland and Wales. We had five or six coaches and used to do school contract work too, which was regular work and was important through the winter months.

We did tours for three or four different families. There was a local lady of celebrity, Betty Balfour-Smith; we took her on her honeymoon down to the West Country.

The typical journey into Fareham in the 1960s was 5/- [25p], about £5 today by taxi.

Betty Balfour-Smith's dance class in Sunningdale Road. Late 1940s.

EDWARD SNELL
We moved into Westbrook Road, the house cost £381 just before the war. It was sold last year for £145,000, virtually as it was in the 1930s. I was apprenticed to Mr Clem Sturgess; he was the only builder that everyone in Portchester still recognises. Yea, you can go into Noon's and they will say this bungalow was built by Clem Sturgess. I worked in the building trade right up to 1990. Clem Sturgess built himself a lovely house up Skew Lane, on the right. That was in the days when they said, and the Council said 'Oh Yes, that's alright! Build on...'

DOROTHY BOXALL
We had quite a thriving branch of the NSPCC here in Portchester and not only did we have coffee mornings, jumble sales and that. We used to have barn dances. My husband Charlie and me used to run barn dances which were really well supported and we used to have the Silver Band from Portsmouth up to the school hall.

In the Women's Institute we worked together, Kathleen [Payne] and me, and we got the evening one going well, then it was some time after I believe that we worked together again and got the Castle View one going, in the daytime.

ERIC MARCHANT
I joined the Social Club, founded in 1923, about 30-40 years ago and I was the Financial Secretary for six years. It was just a wooden hut to start with, with two billiard tables and a dartboard. It is still on the same site and they bought the house next door and built another building and that is in Castle Street. The wooden hut is still men only. Wives and women have to go to the other side – they can't look through. In 1923 there were 25 members and now about 350.

It never used to open on a Sunday and it was only open Saturday 10.00 to 2.00 and 6.00 to 10.00 in the evenings, until they extended the hours everywhere.

When I left school I worked at Vospers. We used to make private yachts, caravans and then they started a few MTBs and inshore minesweepers. After, but not immediately after the war, caravans were made for the fair people. Billy Manning they built two for. He was at Southsea Funfair.

SEB FREEMAN, *VT HALMATIC Marketing Executive. [Very young in the 1960s]*
The shipyard has been here since the late 1930s and on a much smaller site than we see today and was used, I think initially, for the building of motor torpedo boats and loads of gunboats as used in World War II. At that time it was Vosper's yard and in 1966 Vospers and Thornycroft amalgamated at Woolston in Southampton. This yard at Portchester was referred to as a fit out yard.

JOHN OAKEY

I was a draughtsman at that time, doing design work for the controls – switchboards and bits for submarines – big steel things and at the other end of the scale turning it in to lightweight gear.

John Oakey and his son Paul at Vospers in 1964. In the background is Pounds Scrapyard, later to move to Hilsea, and the Smiths Crisps factory. P510 is the Danish Soloven (Sea Lion), launched 19 April 1963 and completed June 1964.

At Vospers in the 1960s I ended up doing liaison work for the service engineers. Because I had a passport – it was quite unusual in those days – I went off to Italy in 1968. Then, [in 1969] an engineer came to Cherbourg to meet me off the ferry , it was late in the evening and he said 'Can you drive?' and so for the first time in France I found myself driving to Lorient [some 250 km] to fix a ferry boat! I went out to Gibraltar and shut the by-pass valve on a ship and everything worked again. It was rather nice when you get there and there is a horrible snag and you get it right. It was usually something fairly straightforward.

In 1970 I was made redundant and found a job at Elite Engineering and then off to Marconi at Broadoak.

RUBY PLOWMAN

The Gala and the May Queen were sort of resurrected by the Woodcraft Chivalry in 1950 and there was a lot of discussion as to where it would be held. It was eventually chosen to be in the Castle Keep. We insured the afternoon for £60 which sounds incredible now, just in case it rained. That would have covered all expenses. My father did a lot of the background scenery, like building the throne... and the orb and the sceptre for all the ceremonial bits. The dress I was given was a bit like a sack on me so Mum did lots of alterations; she put a row of sequins down the front, because of course everything (to do with clothing) was still on coupons. As May Queen my young brother was a page and a girl was an assistant to me. It was the first Saturday in May. There was a maypole dance and archery. We practised archery in a field up Cornaway Lane.

The war started when I was six and sweet rationing finished in 1953 when we got married in the August. Dad organised a horse and carriage to take me from the Crossway to the Castle.

JOYCE TOMS

I started as a registered nurse. I then went on to do midwifery and I trained as a health visitor at the University of Southampton for one year. I started on 15th July 1961 as a health visitor. We had to wear grey and were allowed £25 a year; put up to £33 a year. I was teaching the Girls' Life Brigade on child care when it came to meeting the Duke of Edinburgh.

As an essential worker, I managed to get a mortgage from Fareham Borough Council and I have been here since April 1964.

I had a caseload of babies 0-5 years old and there was 997 babies on my books. We visited

Beryl Pearce, after being crowned May Queen, 1957.

the elderly in those days and disabled people. Home Helps and Meals on Wheels helped and we had a very strong Darby and Joan Club at the old Parish Hall.

I was at the child welfare clinic for a whole day a week on a Thursday in the Methodist Hall and a doctor was in the small hall in Castle Street. There were two of us there that were health visitors and we had a number of very good voluntary ladies who helped with the weighing. We gave out vitamin A and D which was free. If we were concerned about a family we would go direct to the NSPCC. We didn't have Social Services then.

In those days we had mother craft and father craft separately! The dads were far more gossipy than the mothers and it was very difficult to get rid of them at the end of the sessions! We used to show the film of the birth of a baby...

As a school nurse I visited Castle Street school and the senior school. I was called 'Nitty Nora the head explorer!' I heard about being attached to doctors so I asked if I could be assigned to the West Street Practice with Dr Barr-Taylor and afterwards Dr O'Connell and Dr Wright. We were under local government. We didn't come back into the N.H.S. until 1974.

I once showed the film 'The Story of Menstruation' to the first years at the Senior School and afterwards I must have put it on the roof of the car and lost it! So I put an advert in the local newspaper saying 'The Story of Menstruation' film had been lost. The newspaper phoned me and said they couldn't use that word so it went in as 'The lost film 'The Story of ----'.' That was during the 60s!

COMMANDER ANTHONY SAVAGE

We were married in 1966 and we weren't entitled to married quarters. At that stage houses in the Portchester area were cheaper than they were in Portsmouth, so we bought a house in Romsey Avenue for £4,400 if I remember correctly and we moved to this one at 15 Portchester Road in 1977.

By then I had been trained at Dartmouth and in 1966 I did my submarine course and

started serving in HMS *Alliance*, a diesel submarine. In the next ten years I served in HMS *Finwhale* and then HMS *Otis* was my last submarine, but in between I served in HMS *Churchill* and HMS *Warspite* which are both nuclear attack submarines.

Our children, Claire and Rachel, both went to Wicor Junior School. I was on the Parent Teacher Association and helped run fetes.

Portchester Secondary School commercial class in 1959.

MOLLY LONG [young in the 1920s, born in Wickham]

I was in the Land Army doing horticulture during the war. When Freddie's first wife died in 1953 we married in 1955. I was 29 and Freddie was 46. He sold his nursery at Shedfield and returned to Portchester where he was born and bought the nursery off White Hart Lane. It was called White Hart Lane Nurseries, where York Gardens is now. I remember going into the field and you could look right down to the sea. I carried on with the nursery until he retired in 1972 when we sold the ground. We grew mostly flowers and lettuce with runner beans as a windbreak right the way round the flowers. Chrysanthemums, dahlias, asparagus green for wreath making, iris in the spring and marigolds. We made quite a lot on marigolds, growing flowers from May until Christmas. Then in the spring we grew boxes of annuals and perennials and Canterbury Bells and things like that. Tomatoes we sold to a tradesman at Shedfield who Freddie knew.

Freddie was over the nursery sometimes at 6.00 or 6.30am when the flowers were in season because he would go and pick extra flowers and bunch them up, because he went down to the shops every day. He had a big Commer van. We did employ one other man to start with and then we had two men over there full time. Freddie never got round to locking the greenhouses at night. He worked until 7 o'clock.

We listened to the radio and had a TV in 1963. Quite late really!

The Community Centre and park, August 2006.

JOAN MILES AND ANGELA DUNSTER

ANGELA It was father who hit upon the idea of a community centre and he managed to get a good team of people together [in about 1960]. They formed this committee but they had quite an uphill struggle because Fareham Borough Council and Hampshire County Council were very reluctant to fund the building of the centre. He decided to become a councillor when he left the Navy so he could work towards getting the centre built. The land belonged to a farm, Mr Stride's.

JOAN It was a big gala day in Portchester when the foundation stone was taken from the Castle. It was an actual bit of the Castle, taken on a cart along to the building itself and the stone laid by Councillor Simpson who was the leader of Fareham Borough Council.

ANGELA We used to run functions, dances, and stuff like that to raise money. We formed the Portchester Players from about 1963. We

actually wrote the script for like a variety show and we put it on at Portchester School. And we sang 'Sisters'. The old time music hall was a great favourite. We got crowds in for that, they liked to join in the old songs. We were supported in building the centre by commercial enterprises within Portchester.

JOAN One supporter was the Plucrop factory, famous for its indescribable smell. It was one of Alan Wicker's very first broadcasts on television on the BBC. He had the housewives along White Hart Lane, myself included, and we all had to open our front window then a van went by and he said 'Here comes the smell' and all us housewives had to rush and close these windows, on the television. We were very proud of ourselves.

I have here the Centre's weekly programme for summer 1966: Monday afternoon – dressmaking class; Monday evening – model boat club social evening; Tuesday afternoon – whist, evening – pigeon club and old time dancing. We think that was Betty Balfour-Smith. Wednesday – netball and evening – camera club, badminton, table tennis and the radio amateurs; Thursday – chiropody for the elders in the morning, afternoons – ladies keep fit, evening – old time dancing and chess; Friday – children's ballet; Saturday – children's cinema, weddings etc. association dances in the evening; Sunday – radio amateurs.

A night out at Portchester Community Centre. The Centre opened in 1966.

KEN SCRIVENS *Chairman of the Community Association*

The Association started in 1962. At first we had a stage in three different sections and that was for the Portchester Players, one [of the founder's] daughters Angela is still a member of the Portchester Players today. She is also our book-keeper as well and she's in the current production of 'Tommy Tucker'.

JOAN EASTMAN

I bought myself a Raleigh Racer! Smee's the florists at Southsea had an arrangement with Saunders, the market gardener at Wicor House along the main road and he had greenhouses at the back. He was the number one carnation grower so I used to leave home at 9 o'clock, cycle over and the carnations were placed in a large box, with the heads supported and laid out. I would strap that to the back of my bike and then I would cycle to Southsea. Miss Smee was quite happy that she would have fresh carnations that day.

Librarians in the Portchester Library in Chalky Walk, then a wooden hut backing on to the Secondary School. This Library closed in 1984 when the new Library and Health Centre opened.

Staff outside the Library in Chalky Walk.

SHEILA GOLDRING *[Young in the early 1930s]*

I started work temporarily in the old Portchester Library in Chalky Walk in 1958. It was attached to the main school, the secondary school then. It was just a wooden hut. Opening hours were 9.00am to 1.00pm, 2.00pm to 4.00pm, 6.00pm to 8.00pm, later till 7.00pm. I worked for 19 hours a week on holiday and sick relief. We had a 'Children's Library'. I felt my daughter didn't miss me.

We had no staff room and no toilet when the library first opened. Later they built on each side of the front door, a restroom on one side and toilet facilities on the other. We bought Mills & Boone books for many retired people rather than Dickens. They used to say we are academics all week; we want to just read rubbish at the weekends... One librarian was Mr Lever, he was ex-Navy. He wasn't qualified. None of us were.

It was not just a library it was a meeting place in a sense. Everybody knew everybody else in Portchester in those days.

Books were issued with a card with their name and address on. Each person was allowed four. Now we have access to the world. Then, if anybody wanted a book you had to go to Fareham or if not Fareham, Winchester, so everything took that much longer. We had large print books and old books were sold off. I retired in 1993.

We all came to the opening of the new library in October, 1984.

WALLACE PRICE

I started in Portchester as a policeman on 1st August 1966 from the Lancashire Constabulary. I had done four years in the Lancashire Police at Old Trafford where we used to put 26 men per shift out walking on foot. The police station in Portchester was in the back garden 8ft by 14ft [11 sq.m] here in

Kelvin Grove and there were five police constables and a sergeant, Sergeant White. We did three shifts, earlies, afternoons and nights. When I came here there were 5 police constables. When I finished there was only me! I retired in 1992.

Wally Price.

Being here was like being in a different country; when a young constable made a mistake up in Lancashire nobody bothered, here you weren't allowed to make a mistake else you would get jumped on from a great height! I had been brought up always to call a spade a spade. If somebody upsets me I let them know rather than wrap it up in flowery language. I was taken round all the schools to meet all the Heads and got introduced to the landlords of the pubs. I got on well with the kids and talked to them about road safety and not going with strangers. My house was a police house, next door was one and the next one to that. In my front garden was a big board to put posters on.

The power of being a policeman hasn't changed at all. What has changed is how you carry that out. I couldn't be a policeman today, I would be sacked. I wouldn't last a month. I would give kids a kick up the bum, a thump round the ear and when I saw the dads in the club, in a roundabout way they would get to know what had happened. It meant that they weren't going to court. I went into a local store the other day and there was a young lad there and he said 'I know you, you were the policeman here. You gave me a good hiding', he is now Area Manager for that store! Now I get that a lot and they say 'Thank God you did what you did and didn't take me to court'.

I used to go out at night alone. I covered from the *Delme Arms* to the Portsmouth City boundary, Vospers more or less, and from the foreshore down at the Castle all the way along to Wicor and to Military Road on top of the hill.

ELIZABETH POOLE

When I returned from London with my daughter, I worked for eleven years in cosmetics in Portsmouth. I started at £3 and finished at £3 3.6. [£3.17$^{1/2}$p] and after that I managed to get a job in the spares department at Vospers. After about 18 months the Chief Examiner wanted a secretary and I got that and got £11 a week. I had £8 a week when I started. The Sales and Commercial Director's secretary left and I got that job at £15 a week... I was lucky to get my first car which was a red Mini JTP 168F, £570 in 1967, when my daughter was 20.

In 1972 I was lucky enough to go with my boss to Venezuela and I went out to type the contract and then in 1978 and '79 I went to Egypt.

Guests at the launch of 'Strahl', built by Vospers in 1962 for the German Navy.

PHYLLIS WATERMAN

After marriage, I started work again in 1972 at 'Evelyn's', later next door to the Nat West Bank. We sold a tremendous amount of wool and every kind of ribbon, elastic and buttons. We were the biggest haberdashery in Portchester.

STAN HAYTER

I retired when I was 65. I had a nephew who had a hotel in Majorca and he said if I would like to go out there and have a room in the hotel and potter around I could. That is what I did for a long time. I went over for the summer time. I did that for three summers.

VIC RESTALL

I left the dockyard when I was 52 [in 1965]. My take-home pay was £10.7s.2d. a week [£10.36p]. I had an offer of a job at Plessey's at Titchfield which was easily available by bicycle for £14 a week, which made a big difference to my wages. My wife did housekeeping for a local builder in Castle Street. He was Mr Rogers who built quite a lot of houses here in Portchester.

JOYCE TOMS

I did quite a lot of health education at the Senior School. I set up a group in the youth club where the youngsters could come and talk to me about anything they wanted to. We talked about contraceptives but didn't actually give any out. We also did some sight testing and carried a piece of string six yards long so the board could be set at the correct distance! I did colour testing too and unfortunately children that didn't pass the colour testing were issued with a form saying that they were 'handicapped'. I am glad they

A Fancy Dress parade at Frobisher Grove Coronation Street Party in 1953.

don't do that any more.

Another job was to do with immigration. If any immigrant came into the country, the immigration authorities would inform the embassies and they would inform their health department. Then it would come to the local health department and finally to the health visitor, who had to visit them and ask if they had had a chest x-ray or if they had ever had tuberculosis, etc. We weren't allowed to tell them that they had to go to the doctor but we gave them a list of doctors.

I do believe that was how TB spread because, by the time the health visitor got to know about them and persuaded any immigrant to go to the surgery, it might be too late and it could spread.

Babies were vaccinated for small pox which was a doctor's job. Then they were vaccinated with the triple vaccine – whooping cough, tetanus and diphtheria. Now all that is taken care of by the practice nurse.

We had a couple of children with muscular dystrophy. Certainly hydrocephalus and spina bifida was very much in vogue in earlier times and they ran in threes. I suppose now with the amniocentesis test that has been reduced. After 1974 I became a nursing officer.

Chapter Seven –
The Sporting Life After 1975

RON & VERA SPARSHOTT [Vera, born in 1921 and Ron in 1918]

RON We belonged to the Portchester Civil Service and on holiday in Wales we saw a beautiful green. It was a big club with three greens. About 15 of us went along and we were shown how to bowl. When we came back we had a couple of meetings, we used to have garage sales to get the money together to start the club. Vera and I came number 4 and 5. We were playing indoor bowls in the Community Centre for about 3½ years. We then got the outdoor green built for us. We had an old sort of wooden club place and then as time went on we were allowed to have a brick one built, by the community Centre. The club started in 1982. We've got 80 members of the club now; we used to have 110 or 120. We've played at Worthing, Bembridge, Lakeside at Hayling and Torquay. There's the P & D League (Portsmouth and District) and the Gosport and Fareham mixed triples, which we play in.

Now, we are the only two left that started the club that are still playing. My father played cricket for Portchester and, when he retired from cricket, he became an umpire.

VERA There used to be a Ladies League but this year [2005] they haven't had one. We've got an artificial green now. They put in a cement base with an underfelt before they put the top on.

Grandson PAUL My dad helped to set up Portchester Tennis Club, which is still going. My brother Andrew used to play for Portchester Cricket Club and now plays for Havant. My great granddad, that was, originally played cricket in Portchester.

Portchester Secondary School Girls Tennis Team, c1957.

MARK BAXTER

I was born 4th November 1966, I am 40 this year. I started off playing for the school teams at Castle Street and Portchester Community as well and was lucky enough to be picked for the Portsmouth Youth team from the age of 13 to 15. At 16 I joined the Navy and played for the *Wicor Mill* Pub in the Portsmouth Men's League. Playing a reasonable standard, I played for Fareham Town, for Paulsgrove, Horndean, Pompey RN and the Navy itself, AFC Portchester and the *Wicor Mill*.

I was playing football for one of the ships down in Plymouth and landed on the base of my spine and was discharged from the Navy in 1999. My football and sporting days are very, very limited now.

I have a lovely family – a daughter of thirteen who dances within the community and two boys, one now ten and one now eight. When the ten year old wanted to play football when he was about six I actually got roped in to go and help down there so that is how it all started.

I volunteered to take on the management of the Under 6s and to help me with that, I got a coaching course to teach you how to train children and adults properly. Portchester actually funded some of the money towards that and every single coach within the club now, there are approximately 35 coaches, are all qualified to a minimum of FA 1 Coaching Badge...

I am now the Mini-soccer Co-ordinator for AFC Portchester. Children pay their weekly subs of £2.50 to have an hour and a half training, they pay their match fees and every child gets that money back somewhere down the line over the season. The mini – soccer side is from the ages ten down to four or five and what we are running with at the moment is two Under 7s Sunday teams, two Under 8s Sunday teams, two Under 9s Sunday teams and three Under 10s Sunday teams, playing 7-a-side football. And we sign on 9-11 players per squad.

My Under-10s have been promoted up to the A league. They go to six different schools, they bond well together and it is surprising how children at the age of ten actually adapt and

A.F.C. Portchester. Mini Soccer Under 10s. 2005/2006 season.

can be so grown up when we lose. We use Red Barn School for the mini soccer. We train at Wicor with around 300 children on a Saturday. We have youth teams 16, 15, 14, 13, 12 and down to 11 year olds, the men's team, which plays in the Wessex League Division 3, and the reserves play at Wicor Rec or they also use Portchester Secondary School. We try to vary it around the community.

We have got one girls' team Under 13s at the moment. We have a Club Welfare Officer and she looks after the Criminal Records Bureau of everyone involved. Everyone has to be cleared.

We have a few kit sponsors; Peter Stiles of P J Stiles Plumbing at the moment. We have got Autoglass, the SEB and Portchester Plastering to sponsor us and every team from the men's down play in exactly the same colour, the same track suits, the same gear. We are in orange tops and black shorts and orange socks. It looks so professional.

We have the 11 to 16 year old teams that play 11 a-side, all in the same club.

Our club dream is to move down to Wicor Rec and have one pitch with floodlights, changing rooms all built up and to promote the 1st team further. Without floodlights or you haven't got a barrier [round your pitch] you cannot progress even if you win the league. This happened four years ago and we lost players going to places like Petersfield and Fareham.

We have the User Group, a fund raising committee and others to help us. Next season every single team will get one match ball which is about £10 to £11 each, so again thanks to the community and parents who brought all this stuff into us.

JOHN MEATYARD

In the early 60s I can remember a few of the cricket names, there was Wally Walters who was the Captain for quite some years. There was Tony Robinson who was always a big hitter and fast bowler, and a few others. The old changing rooms used to be over the entrance archway to the Castle. I can remember playing as far as possibly Winchester and Rowlands Castle. I can remember Lee-on-the-Solent I think.

CRAIG STAINTON *[young in the 1960s]*

I've come from a sporting family. My grandfather was a professional cricketer, my uncle was a professional footballer and my father was a professional footballer. I have played cricket since I could walk. I am club captain of Portchester Cricket Club, club captain for five years, first team captain for 10 years and I run the sides. We have three sides that play on a Saturday and one on a Sunday. In the first team we have eight local Portchester players. We have about 40 members overall from Portchester. It is not

just the young teenagers that are playing, it is their parents that sometimes come along to support and help with transport. It is believed to be the oldest sporting club in Portchester – we were one of the first clubs ever to play the Hambledon Cricket Players (as they were called) in the record books...

Local people, local businesses help the club as well. Its records go back to 1815 when the club was started by the vicar, playing in the Castle, next to the church. The club was one of the first three clubs ever to play cricket against the MCC, The Hambledon Cricket Players (as they were called.)

Nine months ago the cricket club, as a Focus Club, took over the leadership of all four primary schools (now that number is five) and two senior schools as the England and Wales Cricket Board prefer and now co-ordinate all the cricket that goes on within those schools. We moved to Cams Hall School last March [2005], after receiving an £80,000 grant from the Lottery and the school also received money from their governing body. We put the grant together as a community project. We laid an artificial square for the school to use at our expense. We have built permanent outdoor nets and look to build a permanent pavilion. We are hoping in the next 18 months to affect 5,000 people in Portchester...

As a club we play in over six counties and joined the Hampshire League in 1992, having played friendly only until that date.

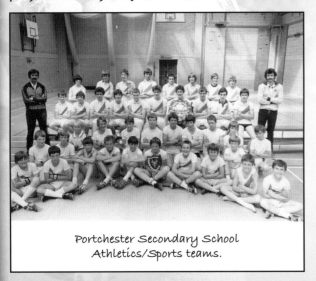

Portchester Secondary School
Athletics/Sports teams.

In my ten years as captain the club has achieved seven promotions and has just been promoted from Hampshire League 2 to Division 1. This league is the biggest league in the country. There are 44 Divisions within the league of which we are at the top of the pyramid.

Next season the 1st team will be playing sides like Waterlooville, Portsmouth, Fareham, Basingstoke – big clubs. For a small club and village like Portchester that is a massive achievement. We end the season with a tour and have just been to Worcester for four days. I am the opening bat!

JOHN & JOYCE OAKEY

JOHN In the Sailing Club you go right through the spectrum of boats and people. People have got vast motor yachts and they keep them at Port Solent. It is a shame that the few yobos that come and do damage, still do that. There is no reason because it is a very democratic organisation. You say 'Join the club, don't throw rocks at the place'. They don't need a boat because the sailing club owns quite a few dinghies that the members can use.

I keep my boat down there. I stopped off with a 7 metre boat and that suits me because I can manage it on my own if I need.

JOYCE John used to teach the youngsters to sail but now they have got trainers and they have training days and they start them from about eight years old.

COMMANDER ANTHONY SAVAGE

About eight years ago I joined Portchester Sailing Club and, when I can, sail dinghies there.

KEN SCRIVENS, *Chairman of the Community Association [very young in the 1920s]*

We have badminton here twice a week, we have karate, judo, we have that twice a week. We have Petanque. We can play curling on a badminton court; disabled people can use it even in a wheelchair. So I'm interested in that, trying to get it underway.

Chapter Eight –
Portchester in Living Memory
1975 – 2005

An aerial view of Portchester with Vospers and Port Solent in the background. 26th August 2006.

MOLLY LONG

I used to go up to the library up Chalky Walk; nowadays [aged 90] I go to the library every two weeks. I go to the precinct to shop – once a week. Much, much nicer than shopping in West Street when you had to cross backwards and forwards over the road. I still have the milk delivered and also the coal. I watch TV and do a lot of reading. I do crosswords, word games and anagrams, anything to keep my mind active. And I garden. I love my garden. I can still dig. I grow a lot of vegetables, all the common vegetable that one uses, which I eat, and a few flowers in the borders. I cut the grass with an old pre-war Ransome 12" hand mower.

Wimpey Homes building the Cador Drive Estate at the bottom of Wicor Mill Lane, on the site of the former Midland Cattle Product factory. 1986.

LESLIE NOON

The great thing I noticed in my forty years as an estate agent was that, even to this day, the number of people that do go out of Portchester and then come back. They go across the world, and then come back. What there is about the village is the camaraderie that existed among the families, the children and the schools. It was a village. One tended to move from Portsmouth into Portchester simply because it was out in the country, they weren't going to go

too far, improving their position from a 2 bedroom bungalow into a Sturgess 3 bedroom house or an Ideal Homes 3 bedroom house.

When the precinct came, a builder bought the northern part of the precinct. In the early days, not only did the developer buy the shops, he also provided free car parking behind the shops. When Fareham Borough Council began to introduce parking charges on the south side they found that people weren't going to pay to park when they could go to the north side and have it free. The council had to give free car-parking on the south side.

JOHN SADDEN [*A local librarian. Very young in 1958*]

I have two traditional roles – of lending librarian and reference librarian. Approximately 15 years ago the issues at Portchester were just over 100,000 a year. That has gone up as Portchester has developed and now it is approximately 140,000, quite an increase. Portchester actually bucks the trend across the county. The general trend is down – issues decreasing especially non-fiction.

I think Portchester library is wonderful, the staff are wonderful here. A prime site of course, which helps, by the main shops and the precinct and free parking.

The computers here are funded by the Lottery Fund. It is called 'The People's Network'. We don't charge at all – hence its popularity. We do charge 20p a page for printout, which is quite expensive.

Libraries aim to reach everybody. Young people do have a completely different idea about collecting information and how to use information.

Five years ago we had DVDs, CDs from the mid-90s, cassettes from the 1980s, so we have diversified and used different media other than books. We're now selling book tokens, stationery, pens, notepads, that sort of thing. We now have electronic reference books like the Encyclopaedia Britannica, Oxford Dictionary, National Biography, Grove's Music. There is another one called 'X Refer Plus' which is 100 reference books on line, so people can access all these reference books from a PC sitting in the library, or from home using their library card number. This information is from edited, vetted books, rather than Internet information which may or may not be reliable.

DAVE GOADSBY

Came to VT in 1975, aged 28, working on 33m steel patrol boats for Abu Dhabi and 37m boats for Venezuela, corvettes for Nigeria, later corvettes for Brazil and destroyers for Brazil. We've had Iranians, Kenyans, Saudis and Qataris watching us over our shoulders.

Approaching Vospers, in the basin a new ferry. In 1985 Vospers built the Cheung Kong and Ju Kong for service from Hong Kong.

We now use a ship lift, 14m wide and 60m long, and it slowly lowers into the water. At first, wood and then steel and with Halmatic, after 1998, it is now mostly GRP – a composite plastic fused with a polyester resin. We now make yachts, military, pilot boats, fishing boats, coastguard boats and tugs. Now I am Maintenance Manager.

Since 1980 we've been nationalised, denationalised, we'd gone from about 400 to 800 staff. The big sheds have been built. The unions come in, but they seem a lot less militant now than 30 years ago.

When I started it was £25 a week here. I came from Gosport on a 250cc Royal Enfield. Start time was 7.30am and you'd sometimes end up working until the job was completed and ready for the tide.

SEBASTIAN (SEB) FREEMAN
Marketing Executive, VT Halmatic

Around 1980 the decision was made to concentrate pretty exclusively on the military and commercial markets and this irons out the cyclical nature of the leisure marine business. Halmatic came here into the VT stable in 1998, moved here in 1999, with I think 103 people. Now we fully utilise the site that is 22 acres [9 ha]. Previous to that, the ten years prior to Halmatic moving onto this site, the Portchester site had been used for some sort of super yacht conversions and maintenance of yachts. We are now building new commercial and military boats and refitting boats from around 4m in length up to 40m. Our largest customers are the Ministry of Defence so you have the Royal Navy, the Royal Marines, and then, in commercial sort of areas, the RNLI is a particularly large customer. Overseas, the United States Coastguard and the Chilean Navy. Our apprentices have an agreement with HMS *Sultan* for their classroom work and when they return to us they will still be on day-release every week for college work, ensuring that they have a well rounded time.

We still build yachts, Moody Yachts, a three model range from 49 to 66 ft [15m to 21m]. With GRP you can build in ballistic protection and they are very easy to repair at the end of the day. Modern composites and glass fibres are designed to last at least for 15 years.

We try and involve ourselves in various charitable organisations and the local Primary School in Castle Street.

ELIZABETH POOLE

I had to retire at 60 [in 1987] and I had a small pension from Vospers. Later I then got the job in the school office at Boundary Oak School, a prep school in Fareham, and I was there for 14 years, until I was nearly 78.

In 1983/84 I started painting seriously and used to go on painting holidays and I had to produce three paintings. They went before a panel of judges for a Society of Floral Painters and was accepted. I think that was in 1996. In 1998 we had the chance to go to Sweden to get an exhibition all set up, the pictures hung. I was out there for ten days and I sold two pictures. That one [on my wall] I painted when I was in New Zealand and it's lilies that grow wild there.

A posse of young riders at the Portchester Horse and Pony Association Show, c2002.

COLIN BARTLETT

I retired early after a hip operation and developed my interest in gardening. That cup is the Saunders Coronation Cup – I won it outright at the Portchester Association Show and the other one is the Vosper's Rose Bowl. I now grow a lot of things that I don't eat myself – I just give them away... I have been a single man all my life.

JOHN COOPER

When I retired I had an allotment in Roman Grove. My wife was a keen gardener all her life. She got the allotment and she was absolutely mad keen. The manager entered her into the competition and funnily enough every year from then until my wife died, she won a prize.

My hobby is wood carving; yew, rose, apple, pear, mahogany and holly; any hard wood. I've done a lot of Welsh love spoons. I've carved three meercats, dolphins, carthorse, kangaroos, squirrels, badgers, eggs, egg-cups, anything that comes into my head. I've got some spoons in Amsterdam, Bristol and the Isles of Scilly and I've sent two to Australia.

JOHN TAYLOR

In 1982 my wife and I went to Germany to visit Eric and Irene my sister and he told me he had been captured in the area of Kleve, in the spring of 1945. Later in the evening, after dinner, out came the maps and we went over it all again. 'Where were you on D Day, Eric?' 'Oh that's easy; I need another map...There'. 'Is that Beneville?' 'That's right'. I said 'What were you doing there then?' 'Well', he said 'I joined as a paratrooper and after Crete in 1941, Hitler ordered that paratroopers wouldn't be used anymore so I was returned to general duties.' 'So what were you doing there?' 'I was ammunition supply to a shore battery' 'And that shore battery was at Beneville?' He said 'Yes, why all the questions?' I said 'No more questions, we really were enemies that day. You were supplying ammunition for them to fire at us and we were firing at you!' Now if that's not a small world...!

COMMANDER ANTHONY SAVAGE

I moved on back to surface ships and had a minesweeper that I commanded, and also a mine-hunter I commanded, and then I was Second-in-Command of HMS *Ariadne*. After that time I joined the Intelligence Branch for a while and went to America for two and a half years. I then went back to my first love of submarines and was in charge of submarine escape training at HMS *Dolphin* as it was then, Fort Blockhouse as it is now. We were also involved with the system of using submersibles and remotely operated vehicles to help people who are stuck in a submarine to get them out, without getting them wet.

Admiral Woodward eventually took a force down to the Falklands [1982] and we were one of the ships – HMS *Ariadne* – a frigate. But we had a slight defect and we came back from exercises off Gibraltar and handed all our ammunition and all our stores over to ships going south and we came back. This was a bit of a disappointment for us because that is what we were trained for. Eventually we did go to the Falklands but by the time we got there the war had finished, which was of course a good thing.

MADGE MILLER
I moved to Assheton Court in 1983, built by Fareham Borough Council, when my mother died; they had rented their house. They had wardens here that were on nights, but now we have to rely on pulling a cord and the message goes through to Chichester and they send someone to help. This room is called a studio as opposed to a bed-sit – we are nice and warm here.

The Gala Parade in White Hart Lane, 2006.

RUBY PLOWMAN
The Access Group started in Portchester but it spread and is now Fareham-based. I was quite disabled at that time, in a wheelchair and it was quite frustrating to go to a shop and not be able to get through the door. With an outstretched leg it meant to turn anywhere in a clothes shop you got your foot tangled up in all the clothes. I was very dependent on someone pushing me.

I undertook to do the survey of the new Fareham Shopping Centre and I eventually did a 45 minute chat to the developers at the Council. They have put in seventeen of the eighteen points that I made. Then we spent about an hour and a half going round the Crematorium where drop kerbs were needed and after about six months I had a phone call from the Access Officer saying would I be able to go to the opening of the alterations. After the tour we went back to the office. It was such a tiny office with all these Councillors in there, so I sat drinking coffee with my legs hanging out the door. I needed more room than most! So there are often funny sides to things and you have to have a sense of humour... I always study all the planning notices in the paper.

JOAN EASTMAN
I had my warrant as a Cub Master when I was 18 and I held a warrant from 1949 until I retired in 1993 as a scout person... with the 53rd 2nd Paulsgrove Pack I started in 1953. It was lovely with Molly Cobham. I thoroughly enjoyed it.
We came to this brand new bungalow on 9th January 1984 and my husband died on 4th October 1984. It was very sad because we didn't have much when we married but life improved. I started at GEC Marconi on 13th August 1958 and I stayed until I retired at the end of April 1993. On the shop floor for years, then I went over to the Test Department. I became a Union Rep and I did that very well... I also worked at Midland Cattle Products in Wicor Lane – they used to go into the abattoirs and collect all the bits and pieces... all the fat into a big vat and then it went through to another vat and it was heated up and then poured in to cardboard boxes. Each box weighed 56 lbs. [25 kg]. I didn't like that job very much. All the bones were made into bone meal.

ANN WAUDBY
[We returned to Portchester in 1983] and my husband was already a Scout leader since he was 18 and I started Cubs, 8-11, teaching them knots and games and handicrafts; teamwork. We used to camp, normally for one

Carnival Parade
Cole's Fun Fair
Arena Entertainment
Flower Festival
And much more!

Saturday 22 July 2000

Procession Starts at 11.30 am
From Portchester Community Centre

Official Programme 50p

Including FREE entry to draw
for £100 cash prize

Portchester Gala
Programme, 2000.

weekend and one week per year at Basingstoke and near Brighton and Romsey.

I was a Guide in the 2nd Portchester in the 1950s and 60s. We met in the Scout hut in Chalky Walk. It used to be considered very good that you'd been a Scout or Guide. I think there aren't as many children now and a lack of leaders. So many more women go to work and stay at work longer. Now you have to tread very carefully, not to be left alone with a child. Adults have to go through the Criminal Records Bureau. I'm now a Commissioner in the Fareham District which includes Portchester and support other leaders, presenting their warrants.

DR GORDON SOMMERVILLE

Here in Portchester since 1983, fresh off the training scheme for general practice. I managed to get the job here [at Westlands Health Centre] with Dr Alan Coppin in a two man practice. Now, we are four full-time and two part-time. We've got about 10,000 patients.

I think the organisation has changed a lot in that, when I first started, we had a morning surgery and an afternoon surgery and everything would get done in that. Now we are much more likely to treat patients in more specialised and focused clinics and would delegate a lot of the care to practice nurses. We have one nurse who is very highly trained in asthma care, another in hypertension, and another in diabetes. We review the patients less often than we would have before. These

health conditions have been growing and we are noticing them more; maybe we weren't diagnosing them as often as we should have before and also people are living longer. The longer you live the more time you have to collect another illness…

We seem to be seeing an awful lot of childhood obesity, which is put down to poor diet, lack of exercise and activity. The telly and play stations and computers are very much more prevalent than they were. We worry about alcohol related illness; we see a lot of it.

We have a contract with the Gosport and Fareham Primary Care Trust. We are a group of independent practitioners, GPs, and we have a contract with the PCT to provide general medical services.

We do spend an awful lot of time and energy ticking boxes. I do sometimes think it stifles innovation and just means that there is a mediocre level of care.

Sometimes we see sickly children who, despite having the opportunity (the good food and nutrition is there) they seem to have been largely fed on junk foods and television. I worry! I worry that maybe there is a generation coming through who are going to be burying their children.

COMMANDER ANTHONY SAVAGE

My wife and I always went to Dr O'Connell and he moved in to Portchester Health Centre but Dr.O'Connell was actually our next-door neighbour until he died last year. We had a couple of tragedies with our children and Dr. O'Connell in particular was a great help to us and support. I went in [to the Health Centre] yesterday for a diving medical because I am going to do some diving again after a ten year break. We are going to Egypt and will meet our youngest daughter, Rachel.

I go to Wicor for Smith's the DIY place, which is a source of great knowledge. I am a great one for supporting the local shopkeepers as much as possible. It has enabled the village to survive and people go there to shop rather than automatically going to Fareham or Tesco's.

NELL WYCHERLEY

In 1987/88 I happened to go to a meeting at the Community School which was held by the Social Services to do caring in the community. Through our church we had an invitation to go. Someone came up to me and said' Are you interested in Stroke?' It was Ann Slade from the Stroke Association in London and she was looking for people who might take up the challenge of starting a stroke club. After a meeting in Fareham with the then Mayor, Councillor McDonald, I found myself chairman of the Portchester Stroke Club from April 1988. We celebrated our tenth anniversary; we had a service at the church and our fifteenth similarly. The problem is finding people to take over from you when you get to the point that you think you should give up. My next door neighbour is a very, very excellent voluntary secretary; we are looking at our ages! Some people are happy to come to a club and meet with other people. I visit those who are house-bound. We start our meetings with a word of prayer, we have quizzes, table-top games, a raffle and visits out, and it is like a little family. We are something like 18 to 22 on a Wednesday...

I think the Stroke Club is very important because people who cannot get out and about... do feel suddenly bereaved as it were; they have been used to doing all sorts of things and all of a sudden their lives and their partner's, or whoever the carer is, they suddenly feel shocked...

We have fun and entertainment and it is social therapy... We laugh about ourselves a lot because we are always eating and drinking. Children from the local primary school are coming to visit us this month to sing for us.

We have had help from the Lottery, Sainsbury's, the local Social Services and Hampshire County Council...

When I divorced my husband I had to launch out into running a bed and breakfast business in 1988 and have to cope with people who come. I have business people, labourers, one had been a successful bank robber (he told me), couples, and one who had a call in the night that his parents and one of his daughters had been killed in a car crash in the States. One gentleman used to come week by week, Monday to Friday, and he was a smoker but he never once smoked indoors. I have had one or two problems but not many in the seventeen years. I think I ought to write a book!

JOHN & JOYCE OAKEY

We have been here fifty years this year. We have done lots of interesting things. We visit places around here and we go further afield to visit places. We are members of Heritage and the National Trust. We go up to Fort Nelson when they have things up there. We are managing quite well. We manage to run a car, we go abroad. It is so much cheaper anyway.

HAZEL WOODMAN

We joined the Portchester Society and soon became committee members. Our first meetings used to be in Bob Munden's house in Castle Street. He was Chairman at the time but because of his political commitment he had to resign and was looking for a Chairman. I was approached and, [eventually], said 'Yes, alright, I'll do it!' All of the committee of the Portchester Society, except for one, resigned in 2000 over the demolishing and the rebuild of the Parish Hall, at the corner of Castle

Portchester Parish Hall in 2001. Built in 1912 it stood on the corner of Castle Street and White Hart Lane until demolished in 2001 after the new Parish Hall was completed. A pagoda, constructed from materials from the old Hall stands in the garden of Box Tree Court which now occupies the site. In the past, Box Tree Cottages stood on the site of the car park of the old Parish Hall.

Street and White Hart Lane. It now has a block of residential apartments on the site called 'Box Tree Court'. The new Parish Hall is built at the top end of Castle Street. We started off the Portchester Civic Society in December 2000 and it has grown from some 50 members and now has a very supportive membership.

NICOLE MATTRAVERS [born in February 1995]

I'm in Year 6 at Red Barn School. Art is my favourite subject. We do some drawing, illustrations of books. I might be an artist or I'd like to be a vet, 'cos I like animals. Dogs are my favourite and at home I've got two cats. In literacy we're on a topic with whales and writing a report, how they breathe and they're found in every ocean.

There are 20 in my class. We share computers. We learn maths using number lines from 1 to 100 and you have to make a number, make all the numbers add up to 100. We did fractions in Year 5 and percentages in Year 6. We're learning about World War 2, about people that have been evacuated. The Germans were bombing England and [children] had to go to another country – the countryside – and their mums and dads had to stay 'cos the women had to do war jobs.

We've just come back from Kingswood Activity Centre near Bembridge. We did some caving, had to make a movie with a cuddly toy monkey. We loved the food.

A professional comes in to teach us cricket, I'm right handed. At home I play computer games and Play Station games. On birthdays I have a sleep-over or go to the cinema and have a meal at McDonalds. On weekends I go to bed at 10 o'clock.

I like being a Year 6 girl because you're the oldest in the school and you need to set an example.

JOSEPH RINOMHOTA [born in May 1995]

In Year 6 [at Red Barn Primary School] maths is my favourite subject. In English we had to write a report on spiders, they have eight legs. We play football and tag rugby, football taught by our PE teacher and an adult comes in and teaches us tag rugby. I don't support Pompey.

Castle Street looking north. 1982.

At Kingswood on the Isle-of-Wight we did go-karting, problem solving and archery. The kart had an engine. At home I play computer games and play in the street, have friends round to play and birthdays are teas at home. I have a TV in my bedroom, Mum controls the on/off switch.

MARTIN TURP [born in 1987]

My grandfather was part of the Portchester Fire Station, my father is now at the Fire Station, a retained fire fighter it is called. My parents moved here in 1985 and I was born in 1987. I went to Castle Primary first and then Portchester Community School. It was a very radical change from sitting in a classroom all day and having to move to different rooms around the school. We had an emblem of Portchester Castle on our jumpers. When Miss Ewen took over as Head the old jumpers were scrapped and Portchester just became a name. To me it lost its identity.

My father works at Vosper Thornycroft and my mother works at Red Barn School and we live in a Sturgess built house. After school I worked for two years for an internet provider at Cams Hall Estate on the help desk; the experience is very valuable to me.

I am studying Law, Biology, Psychology and Citizenship. In Citizenship I have debates with Phil (Marlow). We are on different sides of the table! We go to college sharing cars. There is a lot of intimidating behaviour so the only time I walk is if I am walking back from my friend's house around the corner. I drive everywhere in Portchester especially at night because I don't feel safe.

PHIL MARLOW [born in 1987]

I went to Northern Infants and Junior and then on to Portchester Community School. Mr Burrows was the head at the junior school and then it changed to Mrs Fane who has done a wonderful job and is still there I believe. Two head teachers at Portchester; Mrs West, she was very much part of the school; Miss Ewen she was very much hidden away, from a student's point of view.

I'm from a musical family and I play the piano, keyboard and bass guitar as well. I was in the swing band for the last school year and I actually won the musical trophy at the end of the year.

My Mum is self-employed as a chartered accountant and she founded her business in 1991. She is in the precinct and my Dad is a self employed plumber and gas fitter. I have to sort out her computers and stuff. That has helped me because at College [in Gosport] I am following Computing. Part of my project is writing a programme to help my Dad make things easier when he is plumbing. I am also doing Sociology, Geography and Citizenship as well. I have applied to Sussex, Surrey and Southampton Universities.

[Vandals] have attempted to break into my mother's a few times. They have never taken anything. The police were called out. My parents both had flu so I had to go down and see that the police got there.

Thatched cottage, Castle Street.
Burnt down in 1988 and rebuilt.

RICHARD HALES

I am Head of a Primary School and a pre-school that takes children from the age of two years and nine months and we take them at the age of five up to the age of eleven. I was trained at the Portsmouth College of Education as it was then and I came to Red Barn as Deputy in 1989 and became Head in January 1991. Currently we have 167 children in the school itself and the pre-school has approximately 60 children on the books but we have only 24 children as a maximum in any one session. The numbers at Red Barn actually are on the increase and we estimate that in January [2006] we should have over 170. We've had small classes which we've been just able to afford. Those classes are now filling up. Most of the ten support staff are part-time. Two are full time mainly because they work with children who have special educational needs.

A third of our pupils actually live in the catchment areas of ten other Hampshire schools which is interesting, as far west as Harrison Primary School in Fareham, some in Gosport and we even have children as far east as living in Havant because their parents work over this way.

Since September 2005 every teacher is entitled to 10% of their teaching time away from class for planning, preparation and assessment. That was a huge change and I've obviously got to provide that class with someone to educate them for those afternoons. That was introduced to address the difficulty that lots of schools including this one have experienced over the last five years or so where teachers have either been very difficult to recruit or they have decided to leave the profession... because the workload is so demanding. They also spend their evenings and their Sundays planning and preparing. That is not a satisfactory working life because people have got families and they're entitled to recharge their batteries...

When I first came to Red Barn the very first national curriculum document had been produced and that, I think, was for science. At least twice since then the national curriculum has been slimmed down. We have to legally assess children at seven and at eleven and when that was first introduced we were expected to test seven year olds in virtually every subject of the curriculum and it was crazy because people could just not cope... It's now just maths, English and science.

The publication of test results, league tables [has put a] lot of pressure on schools, teachers, and head teachers to improve the standards achieved by children. We are inspected by Ofsted and have had extra government money for four interactive white boards that have a built in keyboard. In addition to our budget allocation we have what are called standards funds for different purposes and one of these purposes is to upgrade our computer infrastructure and replace computer equipment.

The Parent Teachers Association is very supportive and very active and is made up of a very small group of parents.

We have links with outside bodies. Julie Biddlecombe, curator of Westbury Manor Museum in Fareham, recently did a project to do with children writing and it was based around a Victorian workhouse. We also have an ongoing partnership with the Royal

The Catholic Church of Our Lady of Walsingham in White Hart Lane, August 2006. Built in 1954.

Armouries Museum at Fort Nelson; last year they ran a history club every Tuesday afternoon for some of our pupils.

We're very proud that St Mary's Church come and run assemblies for us every month in a way that the children, I think, find very enjoyable and easy to understand.

VIC RESTALL

On 3rd August 2005 we will have been married for 70 years and it has been 70 happy years. Unfortunately now my wife is disabled and is in a nursing home along the Fareham Road, where I visit three times a week. My daughter comes and takes me by car.

Red Barn School 2007.

Portchester Castle, August 2006.

KEN SCRIVENS at the Community Association
The jobs I do are all voluntary. I'm retired and I feel I should give something back to the area I have lived in. I've done duties here until 11/12 o'clock at night. I've been here at 6 o'clock in the morning. I've cleaned toilets, unblocked toilets. These days in the Community Centre we have old time dances, tea dances. We have sequence dancing; we have whist, bridge, alcoholics anonymous – they come over here. We have the Temple School of Dancing. Janet Temple was one of Betty Balfour-Smith's pupils – hers is a very respected name in the youngsters' dancing world. On Sundays and Mondays there's a luncheon club.

Some birthday parties are really lovely and there are a number of centres around here which you say are not 'child friendly'. One 16 year old's party we had caused £4,500 worth of damage.

Our biggest problem is youngsters. When you've got 40 marauding youngsters, 12 years to 14 years old, it does put people off coming to the Centre. I don't know what the answer is. I'm going to a meeting... to discuss with the Council and members of the police about the problems of the youth in Portchester. What can we do with them? We just don't know. I am an unpaid volunteer and ... the experts are not coming up with anything.

The police can move them on but within five minutes we've got another group growing. As you've seen tonight young teenagers have been running amok in the park outside. We try, we would like more activities for young people but they are proving a bit difficult. A lack of parental control!

BARBARA WATSON
I would talk to everybody or say 'Hello', you know. You can go out now and I don't know hardly a soul, it is so different. You could leave your doors open. You can't say anything to the girls today if they're swearing, they will swear back – this is your future mothers and fathers – I shan't be here to see it and I don't want to be.

RUBY FRANKUM
I am 83 this year. A lot of changes, a lot of development, there is hardly a green space left. We have everything we need here really, the shops we need, there are plenty of social activities going on, there is education. I am very happy here. This is my home. I am a native. I still meet people that I went to school with. After my mother died, that is when I applied for Council accommodation and I preferred to go to Garden Court and I can remember when this was built. That was in 1978. I have been here 14 years so it has been going on now 27 years. It is lovely here in Garden Court, there is lots of traffic but I don't mind the noise of the traffic. It is alive out there isn't it?

Portchester from the east, c1986.